The Bible Revisited

THE BIBLE
REVISITED

Collected Essays

by George Savitt
(Phil Ossofer)

Library of Congress Cataloging- in- Publication Data
Savitt, George.
The Bible revisited: collected essays/
by George Savitt (Phil Ossofer).
p. cm.

Newspaper columns originally published in the *Miami Times* under the author's pseudonym. Phil Ossofer.
Includes bibliographical references.
1. Bible—Baha'i interpretations 2. Baha'i Faith—Doctrines.
I. Title.
BP377.S28 1991
297'.93—dc20   90-46537
                                                      CIP

ISBN 0-87961-215-0: $ 8.95 (pbk.)

Naturegraph Publishers, Inc.
3543 Indian Creek Road
Happy Camp, CA 96039
U.S.A.

To Mr. Garth C. Reeves, Sr.,
Editor and Publisher of The Miami Times,

without whose friendship and encouragement the columns,
and therefore this book, would not have materialized.

Table of Contents

vi

vii

Preface

The Bible Revisited is the result of a study of religion that began in 1950, when I was forty years old. At that time I read several books on positive thinking. Realizing that such thinking was, in reality, faith, I was inspired to turn to the Bible (a gift from my father), in which I had no interest until that time. It had remained on my bookshelf, unopened, for several years.

My study of the Bible revealed to me insights that did not agree with the usual interpretations as taught in synagogues and churches. Therefore I embarked on an independent investigation for the truth. This investigation led me to the teachings of the Bahá'í Faith, the scriptures of which offered interpretations of the Bible palatable to my inquiring mind. The Bahá'í Faith also provided teachings befitting this universal age. In this day mankind is able to grasp the knowledge of which Jesus spoke, when he said, "I have many things to say unto you, but ye cannot bear them now."

It was in my capacity as public information representative for the local Bahá'í Assembly that I met Mr. Garth C. Reeves, Sr., Editor and Publisher of *The Miami Times*, in 1955. This contact led to the inception of the "Phil Ossofer" column about three years later. *The Bible Revisited* is the fruit of all those years of study and meditation. Thanks to Mrs. Barbara Brown of Naturegraph Publishers, who encouraged me to publish these columns, and her son, Keven Brown, who has compiled and edited them, this work is able to appear in its present form.

It has been said that it is conceit for a columnist to publish his work in book form, as if to suggest that a newspaper column, a fleeting medium by definition, could have lasting significance. I believe, however, that subjects of a spiritual nature are eternally in style. Religious truth is not absolute, but relative; and Divine Revelation is a continuous progressive process. The Bahá'í Faith, revealed in the middle of the last century, contains the latest (but not the last) stage in the progressive revelation of religion, offering guidance for mankind in these troubled times.

This is not a day when one should blindly accept the interpretations of others, no matter how well versed those interpreters are in religious teachings. One's belief should come from one's own heart. Thus, the purpose of this book is to encourage each reader who is searching for answers befitting this universal age to be inspired, as I was, to make his or her own independent investigation for truth.

George Savitt
February 1989

9

The Existence of God

"Have You Ever Seen God?"

I often listen to night talk shows on the radio, being interested in programs covering religion in one form or another. Recently there was a young atheist being interviewed by the talk show host.

Speaking to a caller, the young man asked, "Have you ever seen God?" To me, it was a silly question. With all due respect for his God-less belief, I knew there were things that he believed in that he couldn't see. He has never seen atoms, or the whirling of the earth on its axis at about 1,000 miles an hour. I'm sure he believes in both.

People find it difficult to believe in spiritual things because they can't see them: "because they seeing, see not" (Matthew 13:13). God may be the most hidden of the hidden, but He is also the most manifest of the manifest through the evidences of His work. Consider electricity, for instance. It has been around since the beginning of time, but was unknown until men discovered it. Think of the sun. Powerful as it is, it cannot move one iota from its predetermined orbit. Can one say it wasn't created, but just happened?

I am reminded of the story of Colonel Robert Ingersoll, a noted philosopher and agnostic. While visiting his friend, the Reverend Henry Ward Beecher, he noticed a beautiful globe portraying the constellations and stars of the heavens. After examining it, he asked, "This is just what I have been looking for. Who made it?" "Who made it?" repeated Beecher in simulated astonishment. "Why, nobody made it; it just happened."

Some people don't believe in God because they can't see Him. Well, I can't see or even visualize Him, either, but I do believe! There are evidences of His existence all over the earth. The miracle of life itself is proof of His existence. It seems strange to me how we take so many miraculous things for granted. I was guilty of that myself until I found God. (He really found me!)

Modern science has revealed, and continues to reveal, God's miracles on earth. Electricity has always been here, hidden until science coaxed it out of its isolation. Electricity reminds me of God. Like God, no one has ever seen it, and it is powerful. In order to benefit from this power we must be "plugged in," using a cord. In order to benefit from the power of God, we must be "plugged in" to His prophets, who bring us His "electricity"—His love. And in order to have His love, we must love Him. "They shall prosper that love thee" (Psalm 122:6).

Faith in Non-Physical Realities

The most important things in life have to be taken on faith, such as the idea of a Creator or of a life after death. People have all kinds of ideas ranging from non-belief to full acceptance of a Creator and future life. One must have faith to believe in these things. Paul explained, "Now faith is the substance of things hoped for, the evidence of things not seen" (Hebrews 11:1).

It is difficult to explain a Creator who is unseen and who has always existed, yet there is a physical example that also cannot be explained. I am referring to space. Who can say there is a beginning or an end to space? And if space wasn't always there, what took its place beforehand? An atheist will tell you he doesn't believe in anything he can't see, yet he usually accepts scientific explanations regarding the source of matter, which is invisible and non-perceptible. One atheist told me that science was the creator.

Some of those who cannot accept a belief in life after death say, "There is not enough room for everybody there." But the spiritual world is devoid of time and space. It is after the nature of intellectual realities, such as thought, knowledge, love, happiness, and grief, which take up no space and are imperceptible to the senses. If they did consume space, humans would look like unworldly creatures, with heads much larger than their bodies.

The day will come when each of us will learn the truth about the above subjects.

The Nature of God

People have different concepts of what or who God is. Some believe (1) that He does not exist, (2) that He is dead, (3) that He is an old white-bearded man wearing a crown and sitting on a throne somewhere up in the sky, and (4) that He comes to earth in human form.

I personally believe that we cannot know God at all. I'll explain why I discount the above concepts of God. Does He exist? Well, everything that is created carries solid evidence that there is a creator involved. I marvel at the human body with its intricacies. Do human beings just happen? No way, I say!

If God were dead, being the Creator, He could no longer create. We would all be dead, too, because if He died, the sun would quit sending out its life-giving rays, which keep us alive and make our earth productive. However, from the spiritual point of view, men can be living on earth and yet be dead. Jesus explained this when he said, "Let the dead bury their dead" (Matthew 8:22). God is the spiritual sun, and He does not reach those who disbelieve in Him. It is of these that Jesus spoke.

God cannot be represented as an old white-bearded man

bearing a crown and sitting on a throne up in the sky. Heaven is not a place, it is a condition, which we can attain while on earth.

The Bible assures us that we can have no concept of God. In Psalm 145:3, it is written, "Great is the Lord and greatly to be praised, and his greatness is unsearchable." In Romans 11:33, Paul says, "How unsearchable are his judgments, and his ways past finding out!" Even the Athenians, who worshiped many gods, had an altar inscribed, "To the unknown God" (Acts 17:23).

We cannot know God in His essence, but only through His attributes, as they are mirrored to us in nature, or even more perfectly reflected to us in the deeds of His chosen messengers or prophets.

How God Makes Himself Known

Although there is but one God, people have different ideas of what He is like. Personally, I feel that there is little we can really know of God in essence because He is so far above us that we can have no comprehension of Him. However, because He is our Creator, He makes sure that there is a way by which we can become conscious of Him.

Consciousness of Him, I believe, is attained through knowledge of His attributes, such as mercy, compassion, and love. These and His many other attributes are as mirrors of Himself. These reflections on earth have been (and will continue to be) through certain pure souls, such as Jesus and Muhammad. They manifest God's attributes in the physical world. I call such pure souls Manifestations of God.

By accepting these Manifestations—the reflectors of God's attributes—and by following their teachings, we are inspired to assimulate these holy attributes. Thus, we develop spiritually. This process is the true purpose of life, because through their teachings we can make life on earth a paradise, and, at the same time, prepare ourselves for the world beyond.

There are persons who do not believe in God or the life beyond. They can't see Him, so He doesn't exist for them. But reflection causes us to realize that there cannot be an effect without a cause. Some powerful Force has caused the universe to come into being. How can we believe that it just happened? There is no creation without a creator, be it physical or spiritual.

God's Intermediary

If you want to go downtown from your home, you need an intermediary—a car, a bus, or a cab—to get you there. If you are hungry you need an intermediary—a grocery store or a restaurant—to get the needed food. The grocery store and the restaurant also need an intermediary: some form of transportation to bring the food from the farms and factories.

Intermediaries come in many forms, and we cannot live without them. A teacher is the intermediary between the student and his education. A mailman is the intermediary between the sender and the receiver. A capsule is the intermediary between an astronaut and his destination in space.

The sun, in order to keep the world alive, has an intermediary—its rays, which endow the earth with the sun's life-giving power. I believe that our Creator, the All-Powerful, uses an intermediary to enable us to become aware of Him. This intermediary is the Holy Spirit, which is manifested in human form age after age. For example, Christ, referring to the reality of the Word within him, said: "Before Abraham was, I am" (John 8:58), and "Heaven and earth shall pass away, but my words shall not pass away" (Matthew 24:35).

The Holy Spirit is the teacher acting as the intermediary between the student (man) and his spiritual education, which enables him to reflect the attributes of God, thereby fulfilling his destiny as the image of God. Left to his own devices, man degrades himself. But through spiritual education he is awakened ("reborn") to his true being, preparing him for eternal life.

This world consists of several realms or kingdoms: the mineral, the vegetable, the animal, and the human realm. Each of these realms lacks understanding of those above it. The mineral realm does not understand the growing power of the vegetable realm; the vegetable realm does not understand the power of movement in the animal, and the animal cannot conceive of the working of the human mind. Likewise, the human creature, man, cannot comprehend the Creator, who is far above the realms of His creation. In fact, but for God's Teachers, such as Moses, Jesus, Muhammad, and others, men would have no way of being conscious of their Creator. These Holy Teachers are, in reality, intermediaries who make known to man the laws of the Creator. What we can know of Him comes to us from these intermediaries.

When they are on earth they embody the Holy Spirit and bring the scriptures, which contain the rules for the game of life. When we accept them as bearers of the Word of God, in our actions as well as in our words, we are born spiritually, and we then may obtain an inkling of what God is. Jesus indicated this when he said: "He that hath seen me hath seen the Father" (John 14:9).

Consider the sun, its rays, and a pure, cleansed mirror. The sun, shining upon a cleansed mirror, gives us a reflection of the sun. God, the spiritual sun, shines His rays, the Holy Spirit, upon His perfect mirrors, His Teachers, through whom men see the reflection of God, but not God Himself. Jesus said of the Father, "Ye have neither heard his voice at any time, nor seen his shape" (John 5:37).

Knowledge of God

Man claims to know his Creator, but his is not a true knowledge of God, for our knowledge of God is only relative to our own state of existence. The Creator is unknowable because that which is created (in this case, man) cannot fathom that which created it. The chair does not know the carpenter who created it, nor does the shoe understand the shoemaker who made it.

Because human beings have been endowed with the ability to think and understand, they are able to be conscious of a higher order than themselves, the one that created them. However, if a person tries to visualize that Creator in a physical context, he merely creates fancy idols out of his idle fancies. Therefore, man cannot visualize the Creator that he knows does exist. Jesus gave us a hint to this fact, saying, "God is a Spirit; and they that worship him must worship him in spirit and in truth" (John 4:24).

How then can man know this great unknowable Essence, this Spirit of whom Jesus spoke? He makes Himself known by manifesting His attributes in human form, as in Jesus, who was an earthly reflection of the Creator. Picture Jesus as a perfect mirror in which the holy light of the Creator—the spiritual sun—shines. In truth, we do not actually see the Creator; we see a reflection of His attributes in the mirror of Jesus. His attributes are perfectly reflected so it is possible to say, "We see God," when we see Jesus.

If this analogy seems far out, here is a test that may explain it more clearly. Look into a mirror. You see a reflection of your face, and you say, "I see my face." Not really! Actually, you have never seen your face. Then, how can you say, "I have seen God"?

I believe that man's knowledge of God comes when he begins to know that God is unknowable.

God's Name

Does our Creator have a name? He is called by a number of names: God, Jehovah, Alláh, and Yahweh, for example. Is one of these names His true name? I think not. In reality, He has no name.

Names given the Creator are merely symbols used to identify Him as our heavenly Father. He is the Creator and names are created things, "tools" designed by men in order to identify each other. No earthly name can be His name, because that which is created can never befit the Creator. We cannot lower the Creator to a created level.

I have no quarrel with any name by which our Creator is called since we need a form of identification in our worldly languages. "God is a Spirit; and they that worship him must worship him in spirit and in truth" (John 4:24). Not knowing the language of the spiritual world, we must be satisfied with the symbolic identifications we can use, be they God, Jehovah, Alláh, or Yahweh. Their differences lie in the differences of language, but all identify Him as the Creator.

Perhaps sometime in the future, when there is one universal language, this prophecy of Zechariah (14:9) will be fulfilled: "And the Lord shall be king over all the earth: in that day shall there be one Lord, and his name one."

The Gender of God

Is God male or female? This unusual question arises from an interesting newspaper item in which God is described as not being masculine. To quote from the article: "It's woman who brings life into the world, and God conceived the universe. Man cannot conceive. God is not dead, She is in labor."

I'll go along with the idea that God is not masculine. But I do not believe He (?) is feminine either. God is too high above our concepts of His being, and sex is but a human reality provided by the Creator to keep the earth populated. God is the Eternal, the Uncreated, and is not of corruptible flesh.

I do not believe that woman is lesser than man or man is lesser than woman in the eternal scheme of God. The idea of woman's inferiority in Christianity stems from an overemphasis on the statements of Paul in I Corinthians 14:34-35, regarding the inferior station of women in the church. I agree with Reverend John T. Catoir, co-author of *The Challenge of Love,* who wrote, "Most of the manuals of ethics and spirituality addressed to women—and written by men—confirmed the prejudice of subjection, and exaggerated the Pauline attitude, overlooking the fact that St. Paul was writing, no doubt with the inspiration of the Holy Spirit, but also in the sociology of his time." Paul indicated the spiritual equality of men and women in Galatians

3:28, which reads, "There is neither Jew nor Greek, there is neither bond nor free, there is neither male nor female: for ye are all one in Christ Jesus."

Is God Dead?

The expression "God is dead" is espoused by two kinds of people. One kind consists of those who have not found Him. They remind me of Aesop's story of the fox and the grapes. The fox, after unsuccessfully trying to reach the grapes on the vine, left, saying they were sour grapes anyway, and unworthy of his efforts to grasp them. These persons, not having found God in their image (rather than seeking His image within themselves), give up the battle, saying "God is dead." That is sour grapes!

The other kind of person includes those who worship God only through lip service, holding to rituals and dogmas, and accepting them as their religion. The living God is a God of action. And the god of rituals and dogmas is not dead. He never existed. One who worships by words alone is an idle worshipper, which makes him an idol worshipper.

An example of this type of worship is found in churches where people of dark skin cannot enter. What purpose can such worship serve when the worshippers fail to prove their love for God by loving their brethren regardless of race or color? Words that do not inspire positive action are empty words. The God of those who are aware of the spiritual life, and who strive for perfection, is vibrantly alive. No one can convince them that "God is dead."

ccccccccccccccccccccc

Necessity of Religion

ccccccccccccccccccccc

Religion: the Source of Civilization

It troubles me when I read about people who believe that religion is a fantasy or fiction. A case of such was a blind poet who lived about four hundred years before Christ. He said that all religion is absurd. My experience with religion satisfies me that the poet was blind spiritually as well as literally. It is a case of the blind leading the blind. Jesus referred to this type of person when He said, "Let the dead bury their dead" (Matthew 8:22).

A study of history and religion reveals that the great civilizations were the result of religious revelation. How else could one explain the great nation that the Hebrews developed after 400 years of slavery and forty years in the wilderness? How else could one explain the destinies of the small band of the followers of Jesus, living under the thumb of the powerful Roman Empire, and the destiny of that empire? We know today how Christianity grew, and how, in a short time (historically) that great empire collapsed. The religion of Islam, brought by Muhammad to a barbarous nomadic people, resulted in a great civilization, which flourished in science and learning while Europe floundered in the Dark Ages.

Jesus was crucified and Muhammad was so persecuted that he claimeu to have suffered more than any other prophet of God. Yet, their words stood the test of time. Empires have risen and fallen, but the religions of God were built on foundations of rock—the rock of ages. They were destined to stand even as the materialistic empires were destined to fall. They have been the true source of the efflorescence of civilization in every age, while their rejection has been the source of civilization's decline.

I believe that out of the present chaos, a new religion will bring forth an even greater civilization, this time through the coming of he who is the "Spirit of Truth" promised by Christ, fulfilling his prayer for the kingdom of God on earth and his prophecy of the one fold.

Arnold Toynbee, noted English historian and educator, said that religion holds the key to the mystery of existence. Until this age, mankind hasn't benefitted from history's lessons, because it has not tried to unlock that mystery with the key of religion. Instead, religion has, to a great extent, been ignored.

Unlike any of the other history books I have read, Toynbee's books emphasize the belief that religion will ultimately bring about the unification of the world. He suggested that we who live in the Western world should revise our traditional methods of studying history. He said, "If our first precept should be to study our own history, not on its own account but for the part which the West has played in the unification of mankind, our second precept, in studying history as a whole, should be to relegate economic and political history to a subordinate place and give religious history the primacy. For religion, after all, is the serious business of the human race."

Toynbee saw religion as being progressive, and he envisioned a Christian-like society (though not necessarily Christianity as we know it today) that had assimilated all the past seers plus the teachings of future seers. Toynbee discovered the exalted station of religion as the harbinger of civilizations.

The Meaning of "Religion"

The word "religion" turns some people off because they don't understand its true meaning. This is in part due to a completely materialistic outlook, and in part due to seeing religionists giving only lip service in their beliefs. Still another reason is the variation of rituals and dogmas, which separate religionists and cause them to overlook the fact that the keystone of true religion rests on the edifice of love and unity. Paul exhorted the Ephesians to be "longsuffering, forebearing" to "one another in love," that they might become perfect "unto the measure and the stature of the fullness of Christ." He called upon them "to keep the unity of the Spirit in the bond of peace," that all might "come in the unity of the faith."

For the materialists, and for those giving lip service to religion or whose practice of religon consists solely of ritual and dogma, a rebirth is necessary in order for them to get a true understanding of religion.

Charles Colton, a 19th century author, described those religionists whose actions differ from their words. He wrote, "Men will wrangle for religion, write for it, fight for it, die for it; anything but live for it." It is because men fail to live their religion that Karl Marx called it "the opiate of the people." He judged religion, not by its teachings, but by the way people practiced it.

When religion is misunderstood, there is a general falling away from moral principles. King Stanislaus I of Poland (1677–1755) wrote, "Religion has nothing more to fear than not being sufficiently understood." Today that fear is well grounded. True religion calls for love and unity, but so much blood has been shed in its name that hate seems to predominate. In the words of Jonathan Swift, "We have just enough religion to make us hate, but not enough to make us love one another." This proves that religion misused or misunderstood is "the opiate of the people," not religion itself.

The Truth of the Bible

Occasionally I have discussions with persons who reject organized religion and who ridicule the Bible. I always smile when I hear their "party line," because my life has become a new life through discovering the spiritual treasures in the scriptures. When someone insists that the Bible is fiction, I wonder how it is that we both delved into this great spiritual mine with the other person coming up with nothing but dirt, while I found so many sparkling gems? It is like hearing someone say that those gems I found in that Book don't exist. If they don't exist, how did I find them? I believe it is because we find what we are seeking.

Such people remind me of the materialistic philosophers, the basis of whose conclusions is that acquisition of the knowledge of phenomena is according to a fixed, invariable law; a law mathematically exact in its operation through the senses. To them, only those objects observed through the five senses—through seeing, hearing, feeling, smelling, and tasting—really exist.

They also remind me of the backwoodsman who, after many years, came to the city and went to the zoo. When he saw a giraffe, he looked at it intently, and then said, "There ain't no such animal." Well, when it comes to the scriptures, there is "such an animal." It exists, and just like me, many others have found it. If the Bible is fiction it wouldn't have survived as the best seller for hundreds of years. Of that I'm sure!

The Game of Life

Americans love entertainment, watching TV game shows, playing video games and indulging in such board games as checkers, chess, and Monopoly. However, there is another game that everyone in the world plays, whether they like it or not. It is the game of life, a game that is played, not for entertainment, but "for keeps." The present condition of the world is evidence that not many people are consciously playing that game by the rules. Many are not even conscious that it has rules, or that there is a Creator of the rules.

Although I always acknowledged the fact that there is a Creator, I too was not conscious of the rules of this lifetime game, that is, until I started to study the rule books—the scriptures. Every game has its purpose—its goals. By reading those Books of Rules for the game of life, I came to the conclusion that there are distinct goals in this game. As I see it, the main goal is for people to acquire virtues, that is, to develop their souls spiritually so that upon their departure from this world they will be prepared to enter one of those mansions in our Father's house (John 14:2).

The greatest deterrent to such development is men's attachment to and concentration on material things. No matter how much they may progress materially they will not be able to realize and express the highest possibilities of life without spiritual virtues. These virtues come only through the Holy Spirit. Without spiritual virtues, one's life in this world would be like life in prison. In reality, it would be the prison of self, for man has the free will to choose between actions that are self-seeking and actions that are self-developing. Developing spiritual virtues is seeking truth, and "the truth shall make you free" (John 8:32).

How Religion Receives a Bad Name

A recent letter to the editor of the local morning paper stated: "When religion ceases to ennoble human beings by making us kinder and more tolerant toward our fellowman, and instead provokes hatred, bigotry, and murder, it becomes an instrument of destruction rather than salvation."

The letter writer pointed out several conflicts going on between religions, such as Catholics versus Protestants in Northern Ireland and Shi'ite Muslims versus Sunni Muslims in the war between Iran and Iraq. I admit that these conflicts give religion a bad name, but why blame that institution? If all the followers of Moses, Jesus, and Muhammad practiced religion as these great prophets taught it, these conflicts would not exist. True practice of religion never ceases to make us "kinder and more tolerant toward our fellowman." It is the turning away from these teachings by those individuals or groups, who either misinterpret the teachings or who seek power, that gives religion a bad name.

The prophets of God do not force people to believe them and to practice their teachings. Free will allows every individual to accept or reject the teachings. Muhammad said, "Let there be no compulsion in religion" (Súra 2:257). It was the wrong practice of religion that caused Communism to come into being. When Karl Marx said that religion is the opiate of the people, he miscalculated. It is the wrongful usage of religion that is the opiate of the people. One might say that he didn't have the right "dope" on the subject.

Conflicts between sects of the same religion, as can be seen in Northern Ireland and in the Middle East, do the most harm to the reputation of religion. Charles Fontaine wrote, "Religious contention is the devil's harvest."

Religion has been bad-mouthed either through apathy or fanaticism, but even as things stand, casting out religion altogether would do much more harm. As William Penn wrote, "If men are so wicked with religion, what would they be without it?" If the answer evades you, think of Adolph Hitler, Joseph Stalin, or other atheistic tyrant dictators.

Man's Spiritual Imbalance

It is my firm belief that the violence, wars, and inhumanity of man today is due to a spiritual "chemical" imbalance that affects his soul. This imbalance is due to his concentration on materialism combined with the neglect of his spiritual side. It is as if he were building an airplane with one wing (the material), and ignoring the other wing (the spiritual). It just won't fly. It is also like making an automobile without a steering wheel. I have often compared life to an automobile, the steering wheel being a symbol of the spiritual aspect of man. It directs him on the straight and narrow path.

I have also used the automobile as a symbol for religion. I believe that religions, like automobiles, have built-in obsolescence. Each is created for a different age. This makes sense to me because, according to scripture, when a teacher such as a Moses, a Jesus, or a Muhammad brings man social laws that fit his age, he also reminds man that another teacher will follow with new social laws; meanwhile he renews the spiritual laws which are eternal. Those who are trying to live by age-old social laws (traditions) are delaying their spiritual growth.

The fundamentalism causing turmoil in Iran is due to an attempt to revert to social laws that are about 1,450 years old. This effort is bound to fail, for the world is traveling, slowly perhaps, toward universality. God's Will cannot be delayed despite strong efforts made by despots and religious fanatics. Dr. Martin Luther King Jr. recognized this truth, saying that racial disturbances were a sign of a dying old world order and the birth of a new world order of peace and justice.

Racial and religious prejudices are the ingredients of a drug that stunts spiritual growth, causing spiritual "imbalance" in the soul of man.

Igniting the Human Candle

Man has a human spirit with the potential to receive the Holy Spirit. His human spirit is a candle (Proverb 20:27), but, unlit, it cannot serve its God-given purpose, that of bringing spiritual light into the world. The human candle needs the Holy Spirit to bring spiritual light into the world and to prepare itself for eternal life. Heaven is a world of spiritual light. Until man's spirit (his candle) is lit with the flame of the Holy Spirit, the image of God that is within him remains latent.

Even as a candle is unable to be lit of itself, man's human spirit cannot become afire with the flame of the Holy Spirit by itself. The secret of acquiring the flame of the Holy Spirit is through receiving (accepting) God's Teacher when he comes to earth. He alone bears the flame, that is, the Word of God, when he comes. "For thou wilt light my candle: the Lord my God will enlighten my darkness" (Psalm 18:28).

"Receiving" God's Teacher differs from hearing the Word

and not understanding it. The beloved Jesus, when asked by his disciples why he spoke in parables, answered, "Because they seeing see not; and hearing they hear not; neither do they understand" (Matthew 13:13). Most of those to whom he spoke failed to "receive" him.

As I understand the Bible, "overcome" means to subjugate one's material desires to the Will of God. Those who do so, according to Revelation 2:17 and 3:12, will learn the new name of God's Teacher when he comes as the Son of man. They are the "elect" whose human spirits (candles) are lit by the flame of the Holy Spirit. This is the essence of being born again.

God's Covenants with Man

In every age God has made a covenant with mankind to obey Him and thereby receive the benefits of a long life and eternal life. "All the paths of the Lord are mercy and truth unto such as keep his covenant and his testimonies" (Psalm 25:10).

At the beginning of known history, God made a covenant with Noah "for perpetual generations" (Genesis 9:12), and another with Abraham that He would make him "a father of many nations" (Genesis 17:4), telling Abraham "I will make nations of thee, and kings shall come out of thee" (Genesis 17:6). God made this covenant with Abraham regarding his seed after him "in their generations for an everlasting covenant" (Genesis 17:7). Among the kings that came out of him were Moses, Jesus, and Muhammad—spiritual kings, each of whom also received covenants from God.

Moses' covenant was the Ten Commandments. Jesus brought a new commandment (a covenant) that men should love one another (John 13:34). Muhammad brought a covenant in which he mentions those made by God with Noah, Abraham, Moses, and Jesus (Súra 33:7).

In the early days of the Bible that Book was referred to as "The Old and New Covenants." It contains God's covenants with the Jews and the Christians, and speaks of reward and punishment, depending on whether these covenants were kept or not. When the Jews disobeyed God's covenant, they were scattered throughout the world. Seeing present conditions in the world it appears to me that both Jesus' and Muhammad's covenants have been broken as well. We do not see men loving each other. Instead hate and prejudice predominate throughout the globe.

Jesus knew what would happen in this age. Thus, he promised mankind the Spirit of Truth, who would come to bring us "all truth" (John 16:13). He will bring a new covenant, leading, this time, to world unity and peace.

Whenever God sends mankind a Teacher, He also sends a covenant. It is a "contract" in which the first party (God) sets up certain duties that are to be accepted by the second party (man), who is to receive benefits in both this world and the next for abiding by that "contract."

There have been a number of covenants sent down to mankind during known history. One was entered into through Noah (Genesis 6:18 and 9:8-17). Another was through Abraham (Genesis 15:18 and 17:2-21), and a third through Moses: the Ten Commandments.

Jeremiah spoke of still another covenant with the House of Israel, "not according to the covenant I made with their fathers" (31:31-32). This prophecy was fulfilled with the appearance of Jesus, who said, "A new commandment I give unto you, that ye love one another" (John 13:34). This was a new covenant which "made the first old . . . and . . . ready to vanish away" (Hebrews 8:13).

Jesus, foreseeing the falling away of the people in the future (as we see today), indicated that the time would come when a still newer covenant would come from God. He promised the coming of the Spirit of Truth (John 16:13), who would make all things new (Revelation 21:5).

The present state of the world is evidence that mankind has broken Christ's covenant. That is why he spoke of the love of many waxing cold because of iniquity, of wars and rumors of wars, of nation rising up against nation, of famines, pestilences (pollution), and earthquakes. Our modern media, having access to news around the world, reveals convincing evidence that we are living in the "time of the end."

Unfortunately, when a new prophet brings a new covenant from God, it is at first a cry in the wilderness. God's Teacher can be recognized because at the beginning he and his followers are always persecuted, many becoming martyred. Thus, when one comes proclaiming he is from God, he and his cause should be investigated, lest we unwittingly persecute the Spirit of Truth.

🔯🔯🔯🔯🔯🔯🔯🔯🔯🔯🔯🔯🔯🔯🔯🔯🔯🔯🔯🔯🔯

Religious Prejudice

🔯🔯🔯🔯🔯🔯🔯🔯🔯🔯🔯🔯🔯🔯🔯🔯🔯🔯🔯🔯🔯

Bloodshed in God's Name

It seems as if most of the bloodshed in the world has been done in the name of religion, despite the fact that each religion has been revealed for the purpose of bringing people together in peace and harmony. This horrible form of religious fervor still exists in this enlightened age. There are still some countries that have state religions which consider other religions in their midst as being heretical, and they oppress and persecute them. It makes one wonder when mankind will become unified and the prayer of Jesus for the coming of the kingdom of God on earth will be answered. At the present time it seems very far off.

Paradoxically, there is hope for the fulfillment of Christ's prayer in the present miserable state of the world, for this condition of the world is a sign of the "time of the end," which augurs a new beginning, as recorded in the 24th chapter of Matthew. That end means the coming of the Son of man in "the glory of his Father with his angels," and he will usher in the kingdom of God. A study of all the Holy Books confirms this. Then will bloodshed in the name of religion cease, for "he shall judge among the nations, and shall rebuke many people: and they shall beat their swords into plowshares, and their spears into pruning hooks: nation shall not lift up sword against nation, neither shall they make war anymore" (Isaiah 2:4).

Religious Antagonism

One of the stumbling blocks that keeps the various religions apart, and often antagonistic toward one another, is the belief held by their adherents that their particular prophet is more important than the others. The Jews revere Moses, but do not accept Jesus. The Christians revere Jesus above all others, many even deifying him. Although they accept Moses as a prophet of God, he is placed at a lower station. Most do not even consider Muhammad as a God-sent prophet. The Muslims look upon Muhammad as being the last of God's messengers—the "seal of the prophets." They pay little attention to Moses and Jesus, despite Muhammad's proclamation that they were true prophets and that their books—the Old and New Testaments—were true Books from God. Muslims do not accept any prophets after Muhammad.

So, it can be seen that instead of having unity in religion, we have prejudice, distrust, and, unfortunately, more bloodshed than in any other area of life. This is wrong! If we believe there is only one Creator, whether we call Him God, Allah, Jehovah, or whatever other name we conceive, then there is only one people too. Common sense similarly tells us that if one God created us all, there can be only one religion, the religion of God.

How, then, can we reconcile the existence of a number of religions with one another? The answer is simple. Each of the divinely revealed religions came at a different time and to a different people. Although God's laws for each society have varied from age to age and place to place, the spiritual and moral values taught to the people are the same. The founders of each religion also told of another who would come later. When he came, the people, in general, clung to their own prophet, rejecting the new one. The New Testament indicates that it is the religious leaders who keep the people from accepting the new prophet (Matthew 23:24, 34).

Because God is one, mankind is one, and all the religions are one, all of the God-sent prophets who brought us the various religions over the ages are also one. Believing this, we must consider that they are one in stature and importance. When the majority of mankind comes to this conclusion, I believe we will see world unity and peace, as promised by the beloved Jesus.

"Judge Not"

I was surprised to hear that the president of a large religious denomination said, "God Almighty does not hear the prayer of a Jew." He attributed this to the failure of Jews to accept Jesus Christ. To me, his statement was presumptious because I don't think that anyone really knows what God does, although we do know that He has sent down laws (covenants) from age to age through his prophets, such as Moses, Jesus, and Muhammad, to name a few. Since Muhammad came after Jesus it is possible that Muslim leaders believe that God does not hear the prayer of a Christian.

I would say that this gentleman is on dangerous ground, for we are told by Jesus to "judge not, that ye be not judged" (Matthew 7:1). As I see it, it is impossible to know one's own spiritual condition, so therefore one cannot know the spiritual condition of others. Some Jews probably live closer to the laws brought by Jesus than many Christians. It is apparent that God will hear the Jews' prayers and not those of Christians who are not obeying the laws. In Matthew 7:21 it is recorded, "Not every one that saith unto me, Lord, Lord, shall enter the kingdom of heaven; but he that doeth the will of my Father which is in heaven."

Being of Jewish birth, I have a stronger reason for disagreeing with this gentleman's statement. At the present time, although I have accepted Jesus Christ as the Messiah, I am enlisted under a banner other than Christianity. However, I know that my prayers have always been heard by God. As a Jew of tender years, I used to pray that my parents would live to a ripe old age. Both lived, in excellent health, to be 94. I also prayed to be led to God's path. When I entered my present religious faith in 1953, at age 43, I was given a book of prayers revealed by the founder of my new-found faith. One of the first prayers I read contained these words: "Thou hast led me to Thy path."

Our merciful God hears—and answers—the sincere prayers of all, regardless of their religious beliefs. This I believe!

Independent Investigation of Truth

All human beings are seekers. Today it seems that most seek material comforts and some, through greed, seek illegal riches by selling drugs or by conning others out of their life savings through false pretenses, such as non-existant oil wells or worthless bonds.

A few human beings seek God, desiring to worship Him by living according to His precepts, which can be found in the scriptures. Some are satisfied to just listen to sermons on the Sabbath, taking no interest in seeking God through their own independent investigations of truth. If all would investigate on their own there would be no religious prejudice on earth, because truth is one.

Jesus said, "Seek, and ye shall find" (Matthew 7:7). John Ruskin, famous English author of the last century, recognized the importance of making one's own independent investigation of truth. He wrote: "Without seeking, truth cannot be known at all. It cannot either be declared from pulpits, set down in articles, nor in any wise prepared and sold in packages ready for use. Truth must be ground for every man by himself out of its husk, with such help as he can get, but not without stern labor of his own."

H. A. Overstreet, noted psychologist, set the same tone in regard to spiritual knowledge, saying, "If a profound spiritual belief is to be achieved by a human being, it must come out of his own experience. It cannot be borrowed ready-made."

It was my experience to find spiritual truth by the methods

of these famous men. The reason I am writing about my experiences in this field is not to instill my beliefs in my readers, but to encourage them to make the effort themselves, if they have not already done so. One's seeking must be whole-hearted. As it is recorded in Deuteronomy 4:29: "But if from thence thou shalt seek the Lord thy God, thou shalt find him, if thou seek him with all thy heart and with all thy soul." The main thing is to make it a "do-it-yourself" project.

Recently I explained my theory about the lack of unity in religion, blaming it on those who rejected succeeding teachers from God. Today I will try to explain how I believe disunity in religion can be overcome.

Most persons of some religious or denominational persuasion are of that persuasion because they were born into a family that held to its teachings. This, in itself, does not make a person a true member of that religion, unless he or she studies it and other religions, and makes his or her own decision. When one rejects what one has little or no knowledge of, he or she fosters prejudice, be it religious or racial. Both forms of prejudice are usually acquired in one's own family through non-critical acceptance of the parent's beliefs. That person may not even know that he or she is prejudiced.

The point is that all individuals, instead of accepting certain creeds from their parents, or anyone else, should seek truth for themselves. One reason many people have turned away from religion is because they have found that the beliefs they accepted without investigation do not inspire them to moral living. They have lost faith in God and religion. People in this predicament should seek true religion on their own.

Have An Open Mind

Being a student of religion, I am sometimes asked what I consider essential to a proper study of the scriptures. My answer is always, Have an open mind. With an open mind, one can weigh the traditional interpretations of the Bible, rather than accepting them blindly. The fallacy of such acceptance can be seen in the rejection of Jesus as the Messiah by the religious leaders of his day. I use this example because history continually repeats itself. It is also possible in this day to reject the Christ upon his return to earth.

All the revealed religions taught that a future Teacher would come. Strangely enough, when one came claiming to be that Teacher, he was rejected by all but a few, and that few became the "elect" of the religion, which came under a new name (Revelation 3:12). For example, the Jewish people did not understand the spiritual symbolism in the Old Testament regarding the coming of the Messiah, having accepted the literal interpretation of the scriptures as given by their religious leaders. Only the spiritually awakened, who were the "elect" of that day, were open minded, enabling them to recognize their Messiah in the person of Jesus.

Today's "Chosen Ones"

The Old Testament tells us that the Hebrews were the chosen people of God. This was considered an eternal thing, never to be changed. It seems to me that the horrible events during World War II disproved such a concept.

It is my belief that that distinction covered only an era in history, during the time the Hebrews kept their covenant with God. As long as they followed the divine teachings given to them by Moses as God's mouthpiece on earth, they were truly chosen people. How else could they have been transformed from an enslaved people into the greatest nation of their day?

Why did they later lose this spiritual status? When Jesus came, saying, "Had you believed Moses, ye would have believed me," their rejection of him caused their downfall, for he also, like Moses, was a mouthpiece of God. History shows that this was the beginning of their falling away from God's grace. This is not a prejudiced viewpoint, because I am a Hebrew by birth and I revere Moses as a prophet of God of the highest order. If the Hebrews have lost this "chosen" status, who then are the chosen ones of God in this day? I believe they are those spiritual souls who have risen above the hatreds and the racial and religious prejudice rampant today, and who recognize that all are made in the image of God. They are the ones who believe in the brotherhood of man under the fatherhood of God, in practice as well as in words.

If I am correct in my belief, the chosen people of today come from all religious, racial, and national backgrounds, as well as those of no religion. After all, God is universal, and so must His chosen ones be.

❖❖❖❖❖❖❖❖❖❖❖❖❖❖❖❖❖❖❖❖

Bible Interpretation

❖❖❖❖❖❖❖❖❖❖❖❖❖❖❖❖❖❖❖❖

Whose Interpretation Counts?

Being a layman and an avid student of the Bible, I am at times challenged on the interpretations I give of many of the scriptures. This is because my understanding of those scriptures differs from the general accepted beliefs. I have been asked, "What makes you think you know more than the clergy?"

I answer by comparing the religious leaders (the high priests) of the days of Jesus, and Peter, the lowly fisherman. The religious leaders, whose knowledge should have enabled them to recognize their Messiah, didn't. On the other hand, Peter, who at the time was unlearned, was able to recognize the Messiah. Upon Peter's faith Jesus built his church.

In the field of religion tradition often blinds one to the spiritual truths. Historically, each time God sent a Teacher he was rejected by most of the clergy and accepted by the lowly, who were rich in spirit. The parable of the virgins (Matthew chapter 25) illustrates my point. The word "virgin" is a symbol of purity, yet according to that parable five of them were foolish. I wondered about that until I figured that the "virgins" represented the clergy, who, after all, should have been best qualified spiritually. Yet, the high priests of that day, like the foolish virgins, allowed their lamps to run out of the spiritual oil, causing them to miss their Promised One. Peter, the lowly fisherman, the lamp of whose heart was filled with the oil of the love of God, recognized Jesus.

When Jesus spoke of the "elect," as recorded in Matthew chapter 24, he was referring to the lowly ones who would recognize him upon his return.

The interpretations that I offer in these essays are based on my own personal investigation of truth. They stem from the teachings of One whom I accept as the Spirit of Truth promised by the beloved Jesus to come in this age. If these interpretations are true, it is an indication that they have come from a higher source, for "no prophecy of the scripture is of any private interpretation" (II Peter 1:20). That includes me.

Denominations: The Result of Scriptural Disagreement

As a student of religion I read about the beliefs of the various religions and also the beliefs of the denominations in these religions. I find no distinctive variations in the religions except for changes in their social laws, which is to be expected, since each was revealed in a different age. They are all related. In fact, I would find It difficult to accept Christianity without the teachings of Judaism because the Christian religion is a confirmation of the Old Testament prophets.

It is in the denominations of the various religions that I find differences that disturb me. Denominations are born of disagreements over interpretations of the scriptures, apparently from the efforts of mere man to interpret, but only prophets of God have the spiritual guidance to interpret the Holy Writ. This is confirmed by Peter (II Peter, 1:20), who writes that "no prophecy of the scripture is of any private interpretation." The Book of Revelation (22:18-19) closes with a warning: "If any man shall add unto these things, God shall add unto him the plagues that are written in this book: and if any man shall take away from the words of the book of this prophecy, God shall take away his part of the book of life, and out of the holy city, and from the things which are written in this book."

I believe that lack of toleration of an individual's private interpretation or the compulsion of one interpretation over others has caused religious hatred and bloodshed throughout the ages. All the prophets of God came to unify mankind. The power of authoritative interpretation and fulfillment has been given only to the prophets. God chose them to sacrifice everything, even their lives, if necessary, in order to proclaim unity. Christ was a supreme example of this. Meditation upon Luke 12:51 reveals that Jesus sadly knew what would transpire after he was gone from earth: "Suppose ye I am come to give peace on earth? I tell you, Nay; but rather division."

The Spirit of Truth Will Guide Us "Into All Truth"

I find it interesting to hear members of various denominations express their interpretations of the Bible. What makes their explanations interesting is that although each spokesman claims he goes strictly by the Bible, each gives a different interpretation. Mark Twain said, "It is a difference of opinion that makes horse races." I can see that it is also a difference of opinion—or interpretation—that makes religious denominations.

Some denominations believe that the Bible says that Christ will return in human form, while others maintain that the Holy (or Christ) Spirit now serves as Jesus' substitute or representative on earth and brings his teachings to men's remembrance. I have a feeling that such differences are the result of individual interpretation, which, according to the Bible, is incorrect: "No prophecy of the scriptures is of any private interpretation" (II Peter, 1:20). Also, in Genesis 40:8, Joseph says, "Do not interpretations belong to God?"

I believe that only Christ could interpret the Old Testament, since the book was long before sealed by God, who told Daniel to "shut up the words, and seal the book, even to the time of the end." When Christ came in those "last days" (Hebrews 1:2) of his time, the book of God was opened and Christ gave its true interpretation. By the same token I believe that only through the Christ Spirit, once again returned in the flesh, can we have the true interpretation of the New Testament, as well as much of the Old Testament left unexplained by Christ. This is indicated by Christ, who said, "Howbeit when he, the Spirit of truth, is come, he will guide you into all truth" (John 16:13).

Christ revealed that he would have a new name upon his return (Revelation 3:12). If he was not to return in the flesh he would not need a new name.

Symbolism in the Bible

Is the Bible Really Literal?

Is the Bible really literal? The majority of the Southern Baptist Convention, 55% of its members, said so.

I find the Bible full of symbols. An excellent example of this can be seen in the passage from Matthew 26:26-28. "Jesus took bread, and blessed it, and brake it, and gave it to the disciples, and said, Take, eat; this is my body. And he took the cup, and gave thanks, and gave it to them, saying, Drink ye all of it; for this is my blood of the new testament." It is evident that when the disciples were finished eating and drinking, the body and the blood of Jesus were still intact. Jesus symbolically told the disciples to ingest the spiritual food and drink he offered.

Consider baptism. Physical baptism does not make a person a true believer. That must come from within. Physical baptism, however, is in itself a symbol—a symbol of one's belief. But as with all physical things, it is meaningless if the heart (the symbolical one!) is not touched in the process of baptism. In the concordance of my Bible there are sixty-five references to the word "heart." Only two of them (Ezekiel 36:26 and II Corinthians 3:3) refer to a heart of flesh. If I were to take all sixty-five references literally, I would "lose heart" in the truth of the Bible. The most fundamental of the fundamentalists knows that a "big-hearted" person would be in a grave physical condition, for a physically enlarged heart is an unhealthy heart. All the real qualities of human beings are spiritual (the kind you can take with you when you go!). After death, an autopsy of the body would not reveal the departed's true qualities, that he or she was generous, honest, industrious, or even big-hearted.

As an experiment, cut up an apple seed. You won't find the branches, the blossoms, or the fruit that are latent within it. To the naked eye, the potential of that seed is invisible, just like the qualities such as love and a pure heart in a human being.

Many of the lessons of the Bible can be seen in the parables of Jesus. As in Aesop's fables, the characters are fictional, but the truth is revealed to those who grasp their symbolism.

Symbols in Everyday Life

There is no doubt in my mind that the most important truths in the Bible are to be found in its symbolisms. Many stories in that book could not be taken literally, such as "the stars of heaven fell unto the earth" (Revelation 6:13). Each star is much larger than the earth.

There are many symbolisms used in our everyday life, which, like those in the Bible, are often misunderstood. For instance, a general in the Spanish Civil War in the 1940s was killed in a plane crash, and when his body was recovered, it was found that his feet bore only stockings. Investigation revealed that he had consulted a fortune teller who told him he would die "with his boots on." The general took this prophecy literally, not realizing that to die with one's boots on means symbolically to die working at one's regular occupation.

Often a symbolic meaning is just the opposite of its literal meaning. If a person is charitable, he is said to have a big heart. Literally, an enlarged heart is a medical deficiency. Black is often used to symbolize evil, but unfortunately, because of prejudice it is extended by racists to include black skin, a physical thing.

The symbolic "black heart" has no relationship to the color of one's skin, for a color used symbolically has no physical implications. In fact, black in the physical sense may be far more important than white, as in the case of white newsprint, which has no real value until the black print is impressed on it. Thus, we shouldn't take the symbolisms with which we live day by day literally. We can die "with our boots on" even if we are barefooted. We can be green with envy without changing the color of our skin, be cowardly without turning yellow, or be saintly ("pure white") without having a white skin.

The meaning of the stars falling to earth and the use of black as evil can be true only in their symbolic sense. In its physical sense, black, like everything else created by God, is beautiful, not evil.

The Hidden Truths of the Bible

My first encounter with the Bible ended in confusion many years ago. I saw the great Book as a conglomeration of conflicting stories. This was truly a disturbing experience for me.

Later, after a few years of studying psychology, a smattering of philosophy (which accounts for my pen name "Phil Ossofer"), and some commentaries on the spiritual aspects of life, a light dawned upon me. This "light," which I recognized as a symbol of spiritual light, enabled me to once again read the Bible; this time with exciting results. This time the scriptures made sense to me, bringing joy—a joy that has sustained me and guided my steps ever since.

I began to see that in order to find the hidden truths of the Bible, one must see its symbolic meanings, beyond the outward words. I speak from experience as one born Jewish. Because I was able to break the "code"—the symbols—in the Old Testament of the coming of my Messiah, I was able to recognize Jesus as the one expected. Jesus was not recognized by most of the people of his day because they held to the outward (literal) interpretations of the words thereby failing to understand the inward truth. Their Holy Book said that the Messiah would come from an unknown place, and that he would rule by the sword. They failed to understand that although his body came from the womb of Mary, the Christ Spirit within him came from heaven (an unknown place). When they heard him speak of turning the other cheek, he who was to bring a sword, they didn't realize that the sword he brought was his message, a two-edged sword that split asunder the believers from the non-believers. It was not given to them to understand. He said, "Therefore speak I to them in parables [symbols]: because they seeing see not; and hearing they hear not; neither do they understand" (Matthew 13:13).

In this day it is possible (with individual effort) for all mankind to understand the Bible. The books of God are open, after having been closed since the time of Daniel (12:4) until this, the "time of the end." Two thousand years ago, Jesus said, "I have yet many things to say unto you, but ye cannot bear them now." Today, we can "bear" them, by seeking out him, the "Spirit of Truth," whom Jesus said would guide us into all truth (John 16:12-13).

Seeing Eyes and Hearing Ears

I often write about the symbolisms in the Bible because I believe one cannot have the full benefit of the scriptures without understanding them. Jesus spoke in parables (symbolisms) and when his disciples asked why, he answered that to them it was given to know the mysteries of the Kingdom of Heaven, but to the multitude it was not given (Matthew 13:11).

Jesus used parables "that it might be fulfilled which was spoken by the prophet, saying . . . I will utter things that have been kept secret from the foundation of the world" (Matthew 13:35). This tells me that without understanding his parables, a person could not know Christ's message.

Christ explained why the multitude didn't grasp his words: "Because they seeing see not; and hearing they hear not, neither do they understand" (Matthew 13:13). The multitude saw Jesus and heard his words, but their hearts were not touched because "this people's heart is waxed gross" (Matthew 13:15). In other words, the people's spiritual eyes and spiritual ears were closed. This can be seen in Revelation, chapters two and three, where Jesus says seven times, "He that hath an ear, let him hear what the Spirit sayeth unto the churches" (2:7, 11, 17 and 29, and 3:6, 13, and 22). Now we know that the people to whom he was speaking heard him literally, but he was appealing to their spiritual ears. His emphasis on this point is more impressive to me because he closes both chapters with that admonition, as if he was issuing an ultimatum to the multitude.

Also in Revelation (2:17), Christ refers to a white stone with a new name written in it "which no man knoweth saving he who receiveth it." As I see it, "receiveth" means seeing with one's spiritual eyes, and hearing with one's spiritual ears.

There are many passages in the Bible that cannot be taken literally. Unless one's spiritual eyes and ears are open the reader of that glorious Book will be like that multitude in the day of Jesus, whom he said it was not given to know the mysteries of the kingdom of heaven, "the things that have been kept secret from the foundation of the world."

"Let The Dead Bury Their Dead"

When I first read the scripture in which Jesus said to his disciple who wanted to leave to bury his father, "Follow me, and let the dead bury their dead" (Matthew 8:22), I didn't understand it. I had to read much more of the Bible to "get the drift."

I found some clues in the Book of John, in which he speaks of the rejection of Jesus. "He came unto his own, and his own received him not (1:11). Then he said that as many as received Jesus "were born, not of blood, nor of the will of the flesh, nor of the will of man, but of God" (1:13).

Now, let's face it. All human beings are physically born of the flesh and of man. What John is telling us here is that by "receiving" Jesus ("receiving" meaning recognizing the Christ Spirit within him), they were born of the spirit—the second birth—and although they were flesh and blood, their lives were elevated to a heavenly state. This is explained in Romans 8:6: "To be spiritually minded is life and peace."

Those who "received him not" remained in spiritual darkness. By turning away from Christ, they turned away from God. They remained in the state of flesh and blood and were considered spiritually dead. This is the evidence that enabled me to understand why Jesus said, "Let the dead bury their dead."

The Loaves and the Fishes

Of all the symbolisms in the Bible, one item, "bread," seems to be used most often. It is used literally on some occasions, but it is the symbolic ones that impress me, for they spell out or describe man's condition under certain circumstances.

One reference to "bread" that many accept literally is the parable of the loaves and the fishes, Matthew 14:17-21, describing the feeding of five thousand people. To me, the impact of this story comes from my belief that they were spiritual loaves and fishes. After all, how much good would it do to feed people just one meal? They must soon be fed again and again to satisfy their hunger. Not so with spiritual food. Once one has dined on the eternal "bread of life," one shall never hunger and "shall live for ever" (John 6:35, 51). These words of Jesus describe the true bread. The bread of life is for eternity, but the material bread serves us only in the short life on earth. When mankind as a whole accepts the eternal bread, it will make this world a heavenly kingdom.

Certain other scriptures have convinced me that the loaves and the fishes were really spiritual food. Jesus, who was "the bread of life," said, "Whoso eateth my flesh, and drinketh my blood, hath eternal life" (John 6:54). There is no way that this scripture can be taken literally. It is the Word of God brought by Jesus to mankind that is the bread of life. The five loaves mentioned in Matthew 14:17 were portions of that eternal bread, sufficient to satisfy spiritually hungry souls.

This is the bread to which the Apostle Paul referred when he said, "Therefore let us keep the feast, not with old leaven, neither with the leaven of malice and wickedness; but with the unleavened bread of sincerity and truth" (I Corinthians 5:8).

More Reflections on "Bread"

Recently I wrote on the symbolism of "bread" as used in the Bible, emphasizing its spiritual meanings. Although "bread" is also used literally in the Bible, we are told that we cannot live by bread alone, but by the Word of God (Deuteronomy 8:3). Symbolically, the Word has been called "the bread of God" (John 6:33), which came down from heaven in the form of the Son of man.

Unfortunately, men have eaten (and are eating) other forms of "bread," the kinds that cause spiritual bellyaches or, better said, spiritual cancer. In the previous column I mentioned the bread of malice and wickedness (I Corinthians 5:8). In I Kings 22:27, it is recorded that the false prophet Micaiah was to be imprisoned and fed the bread of affliction.

The Proverbs (23:6) teach wisdom, warning men to avoid the bread of wickedness. "Eat thou not the bread of him that hath an evil eye." In I Corinthians (11:27) Paul, referring to Christ's body as the bread of life, warned that "whosoever shall eat of this bread, and drink this cup of the Lord, unworthily, shall be guilty of the body and blood of the Lord." Another form of biblical "bread" to be avoided is the "bread of idleness" (Proverb 31:27).

Thus, the Bible has many varieties of bread on its menu. If one lives (or tries to live) a virtuous life as commanded by God through His Covenants with mankind, he will eat the bread that is "soul food," which will never run short in this world or in the next. However, if one chooses the bread of malice and wickedness, his future is likely to be an eternity of burnt toast in the lowest plane of existence in the next world.

It is interesting to note that, in the vernacular of this day, "bread" is a term for money. Since the Bible tells us: "It is easier for a camel to go through the eye of a needle, than for a rich man to enter into the kingdom of God" (Matthew 19:24), even if one has a lot of "bread," he may also have a lot of crust!

Stones and Rocks

Having been associated with the construction industry for twenty-five years, my mind has been alerted to the many references to stones and rocks in the Holy Scriptures. Some references are to good, some to evil; sometimes they are literal and often symbolic. Stones and rocks play a vivid role in religion.

Referring to the good, in Isaiah 28:16 it is recorded: "Therefore, thus saith the Lord God, Behold I lay in Zion for a foundation a stone, a tried stone, a precious corner stone, a sure foundation." As for evil: "Woe unto him that saith to the wood, Awake; to the dumb stone, Arise, it shall teach! Behold, it is laid over with gold and silver, and there is no breath at all in the midst of it" (Habakkuk 2:19).

Stones are referred to literally on occasion. Death by stoning was a form of capital punishment in biblical days. It is mentioned in Leviticus 20:27 and 24:16; Numbers 15:35-36 and Deuteronomy 17:5.

The symbolic references to stones and rocks in the Bible are most impressive. In Deuteronomy 32:4 God is referred to as a Rock, and in Psalm 89:26, He is called the Rock of Salvation.

Stones were also used as witnesses to covenants between God and the Israelites (Joshua 24:26-27). In his sermon on the mount, Jesus described the durability of a house built on a rock (Matthew 7:24), and his Church was to be built on Peter, whom he referred to as a rock (Matthew 16:18).

In I Corinthians 10:4, Paul refers to Christ as the Rock to which Moses spoke, causing it to give forth water. Also Jesus is depicted as a cornerstone (as mentioned in Isaiah 28:16), being "the stone which the builders refused" (Psalm 118:22 and Matthew 21:42). The disciples of Christ are described as "lively stones . . . built up into a spiritual house" (I Peter 2:5).

Speaking in construction terms, to me God is the Architect

who created the blueprints for a holy life, and the revealers of His plans, such as Moses, Jesus, and Muhammad, are the "building supervisors" who direct the construction of God's World Order. Those who accept their commandments are like a wise man "which built his house on a rock."

The Symbol of Fire

When fire is mentioned in discussions on the subject of religion, one usually visualizes its negative aspects, that of eternal punishment. The Bible refers to "fire" on a number of occasions. In the parable of the seeds, the tares (the children of the evil one) "are gathered and burned in the fire" (Matthew 13:38 and 40).

In Isaiah 9:18 we learn that wickedness burns like a fire. Paul, in his second epistle to the Thessalonians (1:8), tells of the Lord Jesus "in flaming fire taking vengence on them that know not God." In the general epistle of James (3:6), it is recorded that "the tongue is a fire . . . of iniquity . . . and is set on fire of hell." Jesus explained this, saying, "Not that which goeth into the mouth defileth a man; but that which cometh out of the mouth, this defileth a man" (Matthew 15:11). With our tongues we must speak truth and words of love, not of hate and prejudice, if we wish to avoid the fires of hell.

"Fire" also has its positive aspects in the Bible. The Lord led the wandering Hebrews in the desert at night "in a pillar of fire, to give them light" (Exodus 13:21). Speaking of the redemption of Zion, the Lord said, "I will be unto her a wall of fire round about, and will be the glory in the midst of her" (Zechariah 2:5).

One must be ignited with the fire of the love of God in order to fulfill one's destiny on earth. This "fire" burns away the dross of materialism, leaving only pure spirit, enabling one to avoid those fires of hell.

There is a third application of "fire" in the Bible. It refers to the tests one must overcome to become a true believer. John the Baptist, speaking of Jesus, said, "He shall baptize you with the Holy Ghost, and with fire" (Matthew 3:11). The early

Christian believers who were thrown to the lions exemplified baptism by fire.

These aspects of "fire" are symbols, for physical fire can affect only the body and not the soul. Moreover, it affects us only in this world, our temporary abode. It is spiritual fire that affects us eternally.

As my readers know, I enjoy playing with words, in seriousness as well as in humor. One word that can be used both ways is "fire," which has its symbolic aspects and its literal meanings.

Literally, the use of "fire" can be positive or negative. It can cook your food or burn your house down. However, it is the symbolism of the word that interests me most. For instance, some people are fired with ambition, but more are fired because of the lack of it.

The Bible is an excellent source of symbolism in reference to fire. In Matthew 3:11, John the Baptist proclaims the coming of Christ who will baptize with the Holy Ghost and with fire. Here, I believe, fire symbolizes oppression and persecution, as suffered by his early followers. In the Parable of the Sower (Matthew 13:18-23), Christ refers to those whose hearts are like stony ground. They accept his word with joy, but fall away when "tribulation or persecution ariseth because of the word." They are unable to withstand the baptism of fire. Those whose hearts contained the fertile soil of understanding remained steadfast even unto death. They were the Christian martyrs who were afire with the love of God.

The Bible also tells us that man's eternal life is determined by his earthly works. In I Corinthians 3:13 it is recorded: "Every man's work shall be made manifest: for the day shall declare it, because it shall be revealed by fire; and the fire shall try every man's work of what sort it is."

If man fails in his earthly work he is in danger of the everlasting fire (Matthew 25:41). This, too, is symbolic fire, because physical fires does not exist in the spiritual world. To me, the everlasting fire is the eternal anguish one's soul might have when it reaches that spiritual world and realizes it had rejected its Lord when it was on earth. Think of the anguish of those who persecuted and crucified Jesus! Such anguish would be worse for me than being burned in a physical fire, for the latter lasts only for a short time, but the other could last for eternity.

The Symbol of Water

There are many mentions of "water" in the Bible. Some do refer to water in its literal sense, but the important references are symbolic. In the Heavenly Books, the divine counsels and commands have been compared to water. Material water cleanses us and slakes our thirst. But symbolically, water cleanses us of our worldly shortcomings and slakes our thirst for spiritual guidance. Ezekiel (36:25) describes this condition with these words of God: "Then will I sprinkle clean water upon you, and ye shall be clean: from all your filthiness, and from all your idols, will I cleanse you."

Peter referred to the ark, saying that only eight souls (Noah and his family) were saved by water (I Peter 3:20). If "water" in this instance had referred to the flood, he would have said that they were saved from water. However, Noah and his family were saved by the water of salvation (the commandments of God), which cleanses us of those earthly shortcomings mentioned above.

In baptism, the water used is symbolic of God's words, for water, if accepted literally, only cleanses the outer body. If one does not have the water of salvation, the true baptism does not occur. That is the water that cleanses the inner (spiritual) heart. When John the Baptist said, "I indeed baptise you with water unto repentance" (Matthew 3:11), he was referring not to the water we drink, but instead, to the spiritual water that penetrates the heart. It is this water that Jesus spoke of when he said, "Verily, verily, I say unto thee, Except a man be born of water and of the Spirit, he cannot enter into the kingdom of God" (John 3:5).

To those who lack the water of salvation (i.e., the spiritually dead), Jesus said, "I would that you wert cold or hot," but because they were not, he said, "I will spue thee out of my mouth" (Revelation 3:15-16). Those who are fit to enter the kingdom of God are those who thirst after "the water of salvation." As it is recorded in Revelation 22:17, "Let him that is athirst come. And whosoever will, let him take the water of life freely."

Such is the "water" that enables men to enter the kingdom.

"My Flesh Is Meat Indeed"

Jesus made a number of references to "flesh," some literal and some symbolic. The Book of John gives a variety of references of both types. Knowledge of the difference between the two eliminates any confusion about flesh as it is described in that Book.

Here are symbolic uses of "flesh" from the words of Jesus: "My flesh is meat indeed" (John 6:55). "Whoso eateth my flesh ... hath eternal life" (6:54). "He that eateth my flesh ... dwelleth in me, and I in him" (6:56). In these references the Word of God is symbolized by the flesh of Jesus. John 1:14 reveals that "the Word was made flesh," meaning that God's Word was given to the world through the human Jesus. We must "eat" (absorb) his words in order to receive eternal life.

Using "flesh" in a literal sense," Jesus said, "The flesh profiteth nothing: the words I speak unto you, they are spirit, and they are life" (John 6:63). Paul warned the people that "there shall no flesh be justified in his [God's] sight" (Romans 3:20), and "if ye live after the flesh, ye shall die" (Romans 8:13).

Life in the flesh is temporal, but the spirit (or soul) is eternal. We must develop the spirit through the Word if our souls are to live in one of the "many mansions" of the next world. Going into that world without spiritual development is like acquiring a car without having any fuel. If a man lives completely by the material life, with no thought for his Creator, and without absorbing His Words, he is like a tree that fails to bring forth good fruit. It will be cut down and cast into the fire (Matthew 7:19).

While we are living here in the flesh, we must develop our spirit. The flesh is the corruptible temporal vehicle that must take on incorruptibility through spiritual development. Acquiring spirit will enable us to live in one of those wonderful mansions prepared for us by Jesus.

"Born of Water and of the Spirit"

When I meditate on the purpose of life, I visualize each person as having been given a spiritual camera with a lifetime supply of spiritual film. As we go along in life we take pictures depicting the things in which we are interested. When we pass into the next world these pictures will be developed and shown to us. If our pictures reveal love for all of our fellowmen, and acts of justice, compassion, and sincerity, we will enter heaven. However, if our pictures show only things of a material nature, we may be kept out of that heavenly world—the kingdom of God—for it is a spiritual world, devoid of material things.

This mental picture of mine was inspired by these words of Jesus: "Except a man be born of water and of the Spirit, he cannot enter into the kingdom of God" (John 3:5). Being born again "of water and of the Spirit" means turning to the things of the Spirit. Material things are to be enjoyed, but not loved, for they can come between us and God. Materialism in itself is a false god. "Love not the world, neither the things that are in the world. If any man love the world, the love of the Father is not in him" (I John 2:15).

When Jesus said, "born of water" he spoke of spiritual water, meaning his teachings. Material water cleans only the outer skin, but spiritual water, which is his words, cleanses the inner heart. Consider John 6:55, where Jesus says, "For my flesh is meat indeed, and my blood is drink indeed." His purpose is not to make cannibals out of us, but to get us to "eat up" and "drink in" his words—words which are capable of making our characters holy and virtuous.

Circumcision and Baptism

Since I study the Bible with regularity, I often come upon scriptures that give me greater insight. I liken the Bible to a bottomless diamond mine in which one must dig deeper and deeper to get its precious gems. Long ago I discovered that one's spiritual eyes must be open in order to truly understand the Bible. If one takes all of its words literally, the Book will compel one to accept concepts that are implausible and unreasonable.

Two easily misunderstood concepts are circumcision and baptism. The Jews hold circumcision to be mandatory. In fact, Jesus was circumcised. The Bible points out, however, that physical circumcision is not as important as its spiritual counterpart. In Romans 2:29 it is written, "But he is a Jew which is one inwardly; and circumcision is that of the heart, in the spirit, and not in the letter; whose praise is not of men, but of God." In Colossians 2:11, Paul speaks of "the circumcision made without hands, in putting off the body of the sins of the flesh by the circumcision of Christ." Of course, he wasn't speaking of physical circumcision.

The same understanding illuminates baptism. In Matthew 3:11, John the Baptist tells of the coming of Jesus, saying, "He will baptize you with the Holy Ghost and with fire." It is plain to see that baptism by fire would be impractical. None could survive it. The fires that John referred to were tests and trials we experience in this life that prove or disprove our belief and faith in God. We are tried daily to enable us to grow spiritually.

Physical circumcision and baptism are helpful only if we recognize that they are outward symbols of inward truths. The real circumcision or baptism is a circumcision or baptism of the heart from all things abhorent to God.

"Life" and "Death"

There are a number of literal mentions of "life" and "death" in the Bible but they are not the important ones, because we are all familiar with the literal aspects of life and death. There is no mystery there. As I understand it, in the Bible "life" symbolically means faith or belief in God, and "death" means unbelief. It is these symbolic meanings that are of consequence. For example, Jesus said, "He that believeth on me, though he were dead, yet shall he live" (John 11:25). He was not referring to a dead person in his grave. "Let the dead bury their dead" (Matthew 8:22) is another statement of Jesus that illustrates this point. Here the dead who are to do the burying are those who rejected Jesus as their Messiah, but who walk as men among men.

Another example for the symbolic meaning of "life" can be seen in Proverb 8:35, where God speaks, saying, "For whoso findeth me findeth life." He was not referring to our physical life. We found that when we were born.

In this materialistic age, many people count their blessings by the accumulation of material comforts. They call this "living." But the Bible warns that "a man's life consisteth not in the abundance of the things which he possesseth" (Luke 12:15). After all, we can't take material things with us when we leave this earth. What we need to accumulate here on earth are those things we can take with us, such as love and a pure heart (the symbolic one!). God is love, and when we enter His world we need to have love if we wish to be in heaven.

By accepting "life" as belief and "death" as unbelief in God and His prophets, we will understand the reason for being loving and compassionate, and for acquiring all the virtues. We will strive to improve ourselves and the world around us. God promises us that if we are faithful, He will give us the crown of life (Revelation 2:10).

The Significance of Resurrection

What is the significance of resurrection? I cannot accept the belief that dead bodies will arise from their graves. According to Jesus, the flesh profiteth nothing (John 6:63). He made a sharp distinction between flesh and spirit, indicating that those who lacked the spirit of faith were as dead: "Let the dead bury their dead" (Matthew 8:22).

Literal resurrection from the grave would not in itself make a person spiritual, because "flesh and blood cannot inherit the kingdom of God; neither doth corruption inherit incorruption" (I Corinthians 15:50). I believe that confusion on this subject stems from interpretation of this scripture: "Behold, I shew you a mystery; we shall not all sleep, but we shall all be changed, in a moment, in the twinkling of an eye, at the last trump: for the trumpet shall sound, and the dead shall be raised incorruptible, and we shall be changed. For this corruptible must put on incorruption, and this mortal must put on immortality" (I Corinthians 15:51-53).

As I see it, the only way that corruption can put on incorruption and mortality can put on immortality is for the living dead—the dead who Jesus said should bury their dead—to be born again on earth, preparing them for the incorruptible world beyond this one.

Abraham, Isaac, and Jacob's bodies have long turned to dust in their graves, but according to Jesus, they still live. He said, "As touching the resurrection of the dead, have ye not read that which was spoken unto you by God, saying, I am the God of Abraham, and the God of Isaac, and the God of Jacob? God is not the God of the dead, but of the living" (Matthew 22:31-32).

Eternal life is promised to all who become resurrected by the Holy Spirit into the spiritual life on earth. The grave from which this resurrection takes place is the grave of darkness and ignorance and of negligence of the knowledge of God.

The Resurrection of Christ

At the Easter season my mind is filled with those scriptures that deal with the resurrection and the return of the Son of man, coming in the glory of his Father to gather his children into one fold.

Literal interpretations of resurrection—that of physical bodies rising out of their graves—do not awe me. Jesus said that the flesh profiteth nothing. The spiritual world beyond this one, "in our Father's house," is mankind's true goal. There the ills of the flesh are forgotten. As Muhammad said, "Whoso shall have believed in God and done what is right, for him will He cancel his deeds of evil; and He will bring him into the gardens beneath whose shades the rivers flow, to abide therein for evermore. This will be the great bliss!" (Súra 64:9).

What then is the meaning of the resurrection of Christ? The reality of Christ was the Word of God which he manifested to his disciples. The lapse between Good Friday and Easter describes the "spiritual death" of the disciples. During this time they were shocked by the crucifixion and failed to heed the divine teachings. After three days the disciples awakened from their disspirited state and began to promulgate the Word of God, which was the reality of Christ. Their bodies and minds became subjugated to the revitalizing power of the Holy Spirit and the Cause of Christ became manifested in the world. This was the true resurrection of Christ. "For as the body without the spirit is dead, so faith without works is dead also" (James 2:26).

The Meaning of Return

Although I do not believe in reincarnation (the return of the soul in another physical body), I do believe in the return of the same spiritual qualities in human form from age to age. Jesus confirms this return in the Bible several times.

First, in regard to the Holy Spirit, he tells us "Before Abraham was, I am" (John 8:58). In other words, the Holy Spirit which was the spiritual reality of Christ and the emanation of Divine Attributes from God, had appeared many times before Christ, reflected in former prophets, and it would continue to appear in future prophets.

Another interesting example of the return of the spiritual qualities is the story of John the Baptist, the forerunner of Jesus. This return of the spirit was prophesied in Malachi 4:5, which reads, "Behold, I will send you Elijah the Prophet before the coming of the great and dreadful day of the Lord." Although John knew he was a forerunner of the promised Messiah who was to come, he did not know that he was, in spirit, the return of Elijah

(Elias in the New Testament). When he was asked if he was Elias who was to come before the Lord, he denied it, saying, "I am not" (John 1:21). Despite John's denial, Christ, speaking of him, said, "And if ye will receive it, this is Elias, which was for to come" (Matthew 11:14). It is evident that Christ saw in John the same power and spirit that had been present in the prophet Elijah, and in this sense, John was the return of Elijah. This is similar to the return of the same species of flower in the spring.

In light of this, it is reasonable that Christ's admonition to "watch therefore: for ye know not what hour your Lord doth come. . . . Therefore, be ye also ready" (Matthew 24:42, 44), was a warning that the Holy Spirit would return in another human form similar to the first coming of the "Son of man," like a "thief in the night" (II Peter 3:10). It is likely that he knew we wouldn't easily recognize that Spirit in any human being, even as the multitudes of his day failed to recognize that Spirit, which had been "before Abraham," in him.

"A New Heaven and a New Earth"

The Bible contains a number of references to "a new heaven and a new earth." These references are symbolic, because the earth does not change. In millions of years it hasn't changed at all, other than through gradual geo-physical transformation.

The symbolism of "a new heaven and a new earth" is that whenever a new teacher is sent by God, the "new heaven" he brings is the restatement of the spiritual or moral laws which had fallen into disuse, and the "new earth" symbolizes the new social laws that fit the age in which he comes. In other words, he makes all things new (Revelation 21:5). This was promised in Isaiah 65:17, where it is recorded, "For behold, I create new heavens and a new earth."

When Jesus came, he brought a new world order—a new heaven and a new earth—renewing the spiritual laws and bringing new social laws for his day. He brought the "new wine" that the old bottles of the Mosaic dispensation could not hold. Jesus knew the time would come when it would be necessary to reveal still another "new heaven and a new earth." The 24th chapter of Matthew describes that time. This will be the day of fulfillment when his laws have been established throughout the world. "This gospel of the kingdom shall be preached in all the world for a witness unto all nations; and then shall the end come" (Matthew 24:14).

The message of the Book of Revelation is the clarion call of the day of which Jesus spoke, when "the Spirit of Truth" guides mankind into all truth, when "he that sat upon the throne said, Behold, I make all things new." John the Divine, author of Revelation, said, "And I saw a new heaven and a new earth: for the first heaven and the first earth were passed away" (Revelation 21:1).

The Meaning of "End of the World"

In February 1962, some so-called experts, expecting an eclipse, feared that the sun might collide with the moon, causing the end of the world. I had no fear because, as a Bible student, I figured that we had to catch up on certain biblical prophecies before the world could disintegrate. The Lord's prayer can be fulfilled only while the world remains on its axis, twirling merrily away. God is still with us and will continue to shower His mercy on us, despite our sinful ways.

Does the Bible really foretell the physical end of the world? William Sears, in his book *Thief in the Night,* in which he presents his extensive study of biblical prophecy and fullfilment, states, "My own study indicates that the 'end of the world' mentioned in scripture was obviously symbolic. It was referred to in some writings as the 'end of the cycle' or the end of an age."

I found that there were two Greek words used for "world." One was "kosmos" the other "aion." Kosmos means the material world and aion means an age or era. The phrase "end of the world" occurs seven times in the New Testament. According to Mr. Sears, aion is used each time, never kosmos. When the disciples of Jesus asked him about "the last days," when he was to return, it is aion that is used. When Jesus referred to the "harvest at the end of the world," it is aion. When he said, "So shall it be at the end of the world," once again it is aion. Clearly, the "return" marks the end of the age or the end of a cycle. This can be seen in Hebrews 1:2, where God refers to the coming of Jesus 2,000 years ago, as "these last days." This meant the end of the Mosaic cycle or age, and the beginning of the cycle or age of Christianity.

In this day, the end of the world means the end of the cycle of hate and prejudice, of wars and threats of wars, of which Jesus spoke. The end of that world means the beginning of a new world, a world of unity and cooperation between the nations.

The Sun, the Moon, and the Stars

The exposure of certain "electronic preachers," although shocking, reveals the fulfillment of Biblical prophecy. The Bible speaks of the falling away of religious leaders, and also of the time when they will no longer be needed.

I base my opinion on certain passages referring to the sun, the moon, and the stars which, we are told, will fail. These passages cannot be taken literally because if the sun were to be darkened, the world couldn't continue to bear life in any form, be it vegetable, animal, or human. Therefore the sun, the moon, and the stars are symbols referring to religious leaders, whose work was intended to spread spiritual light upon their fellowmen.

In Joel 2:31, it is recorded, "The sun shall be turned into darkness, and the moon into blood, before the great and terrible day of the Lord come." If the sun should literally darken, the moon would also be darkened, because it gets its light from the sun. This same theme is repeated in Joel 2:10, Acts 2:20, and Revelation 6:13. In Revelation 6:13, we read that "the stars of heaven fell unto the earth." As I have mentioned in earlier columns, one star is much larger than the earth, which would be completely destroyed by one falling star.

According to other passages in the Bible, the sun, the moon, and the stars (symbols of the spiritual leaders) will no longer be needed. Referring to "New Jerusalem [the city of God] coming down from God out of heaven" (Revelation 21:2), we see that it had "no need of the sun, neither of the moon, to shine in it: for the glory of God did lighten it" (Revelation 21:23). And again, "The sun shall be no more thy light by day; neither for brightness shall the moon give light unto thee: but the Lord shall be unto thee an everlasting light, and thy God thy glory" (Isaiah 60:19). This is to happen when "the Son of man shall come in the glory of his Father with his angels" (Matthew 16:27).

The Meaning of "Clouds"

There are a number of references to "clouds" in the Bible, starting with Exodus 34:5, where it is recorded, "And the Lord descended in the cloud,and stood with him (Moses) there, and proclaimed the name of the Lord." Taken literally, one would believe that God came down from the sky and stood with Moses. Such a belief is unacceptable because heaven is not a physical place somewhere in space. Also, the Lord is not flesh and blood. "God is a Spirit: and they that worship him must worship him in spirit and in truth" (John 4:24). Like the qualities of love, honesty, and justice, the Holy Spirit takes up no space.

In the Bible "clouds" symbolically are those things that keep us from understanding, that is, recognizing the spiritual truths therein, just as the clouds in the sky keep us from beholding the sun. Muhammad spoke of those who were well versed in the words of the Qur'án but who did not understand them, saying that they were like blind men because they could feel the heat of the sun, but could not see its light.

In Daniel 7:13, it is recorded, "I saw in the night visions, and, behold, one like the Son of man came with the clouds of heaven." This scripture evidently refers to the coming of Jesus. "The clouds of heaven" are not the clouds we see in the sky. The kind we see there are formed through moisture rising from the earth. "Clouds of heaven" therefore must have a spiritual connotation. As the clouds above hide the sun, so do the religious leaders in every age hinder the souls of men from recognizing the Christ Spirit when it appears in human form on earth.

"Behold, he cometh with clouds; and every eye shall see him" (Revelation 1:7). The fact that every eye shall see him doesn't mean that every eye shall recognize him. These clouds— "the clouds of heaven"—kept most of the people who actually saw Jesus in the flesh from recognizing the Christ Spirit within him. After all, what good could come out of Nazareth? We know the answer today.

Again, by the term "clouds of heaven" is meant those things brought by God's Messengers that are contrary to the ways and the desires of men, causing them to persecute the prophets when they bring God's Message for mankind. Instead, such as persecute the prophets follow false prophets, who are "clouds without water" (Jude 12).

What are Angels?

There are certain traditions in religion to which I am unable to subscribe. One example is the belief that angels have wings. I have found more than fifty references to angels in the Bible, and only one referred to angels flying (Revelation 14:6).

Seraphim (supposedly celestial beings) are pictured with six wings. According to my Bible, it was believed they originally were pagan gods in snake form. Cherubim, pictured with two wings, were symbolic figures in the temple and tabernacle. I believe that wings on angels are symbolic too. St. Augustine, in his book *The City of God,* stated that he believed that angels were in reality highly developed human beings—messengers of God. He said that the Greek word that in Latin appears as "angelus" means "messenger." The concordance of my Bible agrees with him.

Angels are, on several occasions in the Bible, referred to as men. In Genesis 18:2, the three angels who approached Abraham to inform him that his wife would bear a child, and in Genesis 19:5, the two angels who came to save Lot at Sodom, were described as men. Also, it is recorded in Hebrews 13:2, "Be not forgetful to entertain strangers: for thereby some have entertained angels unawares."

In Jacob's dream of a ladder reaching into heaven, he beheld the angels of God ascending on it. Apparently he, too, pictured angels without wings. Ladders are used for climbing when other methods (such as flying) are not available.

Muhammad, like St. Augustine, described angels as being messengers, and as being wingless. When nonbelievers demanded that he send an angel from heaven to prove he was God's prophet, he said, "If we had appointed an angel, we should certainly have appointed one in the form of man, and we should have clothed him before them in garments like their own" (Súra 6:9).

So . . . when I wing my way to the next world (without wings, of course) the angels I expect to see, if I am fortunate enough to reach their high level of existence, will be those departed human beings whose lives on earth were angelic.

Noah's Ark

I recall watching a TV program titled "The Bible." After it was over I came to the conclusion that if I were not a strong believer in the Bible, the program would have turned me off. The reason? Certain biblical events that were presented as having literal substance could only be allegorical. I am referring to those scenes in which God spoke directly to Cain, the story of the Tower of Babel, and to that of Noah and the ark.

When I was young I thought that at one time, away back in history, God actually spoke (as humans do) to people, and I wondered why He no longer does. As for the Tower of Babel, I believe the differences in language came about through some natural way, possibly when people migrated to isolated places in early history.

The most difficult story for me to believe literally is that of Noah and the ark. One only has to visualize the impossibility of getting two animals (one male and one female) of each kind, when many parts of the world were unknown at that time. Also, bringing them all to the place where the ark was being built by Noah and his family couldn't be literally accomplished. Furthermore, consider how much food would be necessary to have aboard the boat to take care of all the animals and Noah's family for forty days.

Now, I'm not belittling the Bible, especially for what it has done for me. However, the true lessons therein are basically symbolic (except for the recorded history in it), so it would be impossible to "sell" the Bible as being literally true to thinking people. To me, the story of Noah and the ark is symbolically being played out again today. I see the world (and especially America) drowning in the flood of materialism which covers the earth, and the occupants of God's Ark of Deliverance are those who obey His laws as did Noah and his family, and who work to establish harmony and peace in the world.

History repeats itself, symbolically as well as it does literally.

Astrologers tell us that this is the Age of Aquarius. Aquarius means "the water carrier" according to my dictionary. From what I observe around me, I can agree with this description, for in a sense the world is "all wet," an expression which, in my younger days, meant "off the beam" or "on the wrong track."

If we look back to the days of Noah and the ark we will find a situation like our day. In Genesis chapter six, it is recorded, "And God saw that the wickedness of man was great in the earth, and that every imagination of the thoughts of his heart was only evil continually." God was ready to destroy "both man and beast, and the creeping thing, and the fowls of the air; for it repenteth Me that I have made them."

God, therefore, established a covenant with Noah, a righteous man, to build an ark of salvation for his family and two of each living thing, male and female. When the ark was completed and his family and the animals were aboard, the rains came and flooded the earth, killing all that were on its face.

Is the story of Noah and the ark literally true? I don't believe it is. But even if it is only a parable, it has a tremendous impact on me, because today I see a world-covering flood rising once more, fed by the polluted waters of materialism, racial strife, wars, and international intrigue.

But, one might ask, if there is a flood, should there not also be an ark of deliverance? Of course! God sends down retribution upon those who turn from Him, but He also protects those who, despite the general trend of the world, cling to Him and His laws. These are the meek who shall inherit the earth, the elect for whose sake, as Jesus promised, "those days should be shortened" (Matthew 24:22).

The Devil

There's a lot of deviltry going on in this world, and a number of people have come to the conclusion that an entity referred to as the "devil" (or Satan) is responsible. According to a survey made in 1975, 50% of those questioned believed in the existence of the devil. Of this percentage, the survey revealed that virtually no Jews were included. This is because they have not been taught the concept of a personified devil.

Feeling devilish about this subject (being of Jewish birth) I spot-checked the Old Testament and found three mentions each of devil (none of which personified this entity) and Satan. The Hebrew word "Satan" was used originally as a common noun for "adversary." At no time was it personified as one having power over men except where God had ordained it as in Job 1:6.

I'm not even sure that the devil or Satan as referred to in the New Testament can be personified. My doubts surfaced after reading the story of Ananias and his wife (Acts 5:1-10). They were among those who were converted and who professed that their possessions were not really their own, but that they had all things in common. Those who sold possessions laid the proceeds at the Apostles' feet. Ananias and his wife, however, having sold a possession, held back a certain part before laying the remainder at the Apostles' feet.

Peter said, "Ananias, why hath Satan filled thine heart to lie to the Holy Ghost, and to keep back part of the price of the land?" As a result of their lying, both dropped dead when they were exposed by Peter.

My point is this: If Satan were really to blame for their actions, why should they have been punished? If men are to blame Satan (the devil) for the terrible things going on today, where does man's responsibility lie? After all, it is no excuse to say, "The devil made me do it!"

I believe that the "devil" who makes us do bad things is in reality our material nature, as opposed to our spiritual nature. We do wrong actions through our misuse of free will. It is only by giving up our will to follow God's Will that we shall rid ourselves of the deviltry that is strangling the world today.

I often have to explain my belief that there is no being known as the devil or Satan. God, the Creator, is perfection, beyond the understanding of finite man. To me, to believe there is a devil is to believe that there are two creators, one good, the other evil.

Perfection is light and imperfection is darkness. Light has substance, but darkness does not. Physical light originated with the sun (later assisted by artificial light, such as candles, lamps, and electricity). Darkness is merely the absence of light. We turn on a light, and it is only when we turn it off (or when the sun sets) that we find darkness. No one ever turned on darkness. Take knowledge, for instance. In order to gain knowledge, one must make an effort to achieve it. Darkness, compared to the "light" of knowledge, takes no effort at all. The darkness of ignorance is our start in life, and we will remain in that condition without learning. So, who needs a devil to make us ignorant when we can be ignorant without help?

God created us in His image (Genesis 1:27). Since He is perfection, He created us with the ability to work toward perfection. God is Spiritual Light, and if we turn our backs on Him, we see only our own dark shadow—the evil we can choose through failure to make efforts to develop spiritual light. Evil is spiritual darkness, not caused by a devil, but by our own "turning off" of God's light shining on us. However, because of that image of God within us, there is always an opportunity to repent and return to Him. This is also the real meaning of heaven and hell: the former is nearness to God in the sense of mirroring His attributes, and the latter is remoteness from God, due to turning away from His commandments.

God gave man two natures: a physical or animal nature, and a spiritual nature. Man can choose to emphasize his animal nature without the help of a devil.

The Story of Adam & Eve

Is the story of Adam and Eve, as depicted in the Bible, fact or allegory? Those who accept the Bible literally believe it is fact. As a believer in the Bible who doesn't accept creation as literally recorded in the Bible, I decided to look for clues to validate my belief.

My first step was to meditate on God, the Creator. Like the universe He created, He is beyond the understanding of any human being. He is an all-knowing God who cannot be known, "for the Lord is a God of knowledge, and by him actions are weighed" (I Samuel 2:3). He is to be praised for His mighty acts (Psalm 150:2). His law is perfect, His testimony is sure and His commandment is pure (Psalm 19:7-8).

Being all-powerful, it wouldn't have been necessary for Him to rest on the seventh day (Genesis 2:2). All He has to do is say, "Be!" and it is. As I see it, "rest" must have some other meaning than it does when a human being rests after working.

Since God is all-knowing, I cannot believe that His creation of Eve was just an afterthought (Genesis 2:18). Furthermore, I cannot picture a snake talking (3:1) or the marriage of Cain (4:17). If Adam and Eve were the first people on earth, there would have been no one for him to marry.

Now, don't get the idea that I am belittling the Bible. I owe my present belief in God to that great book. To me the story of Adam and Eve is symbolic. A true study of that Book calls for the seeking out of those items which cannot reasonably be taken literally. Paul Tillich, the noted theologian, explained this matter, saying, "Man's ultimate concern must be expressed symbolically, because symbolic language alone is able to express the ultimate."

Miracles

How important are miracles in influencing a person's belief in God? A few persons may have become believers because the miracles performed by Jesus convinced them of his divinity. However, from my study of the Bible, I have concluded that miracles are not really as impressive as they appear on the surface. The significance of Christ's appearance on earth was his power to transform the lives of men through his teachings. The fantastic growth of Christianity since his crucifixion is proof enough of his divinity.

Jesus refused to perform miracles to ease conditions for himself or for the purpose of conversion. He would not turn stones into bread (Luke 4:3), or give the Pharisees a sign of his divinity (Matthew 12:38-39).

When he healed the ten lepers, only one glorified God and thanked him. He said, "Were there not ten cleansed? But where are the nine? There are not found that returned to give glory to God, save this stranger" (Luke 17:17-18).

When Thomas refused to believe without the proof of a wonder, Jesus rebuked him, saying, "Thomas, because thou hast seen me, thou hast believed: blessed are they that have not seen, and yet have believed" (John 20:29). Thus, we can see that Jesus placed no emphasis on miracles. John mentioned the insignificance of miracles, saying, "But though he had done so many miracles before them, yet they believed not on him" (John 12:37).

Christ's mission on earth was to draw men nearer to God through their own volition, not through his outward compulsion. A belief in God is based on understanding, not mystification. Religious history clearly shows that miracles have never been the means of changing the hearts of men. God wants mankind to turn to Him through love, not through miracles. In fact, when one develops a love for all mankind, the change made in his or her life will be truly miraculous. If you really need a miracle, remember that God's love for us (which was the reason He created us) is the greatest miracle of all.

In a previous column I wrote of my belief that miracles are

an insignificant part of religion. Now I am examining miracles to show that they are not always signs from God.

I believe that what we call miracles are the result of natural laws which, because of our spiritual immaturity, we are as yet unable to understand. My dictionary describes a miracle as "an event or effect in the physical world deviating from the known laws of nature, or transcending our knowledge of these laws." Mary Baker Eddy, founder of Christian Science, referred to a miracle as being "that which is divinely natural, but must be learned humanly."

Jesus placed his miraculous works on a human plane when he said, "Verily, verily, I say unto you, He that believeth on me, the works that I do shall he do also; and greater works than these shall he do; because I go unto my Father" (John 14:12). Thus, my argument that miracles do not warrant the attention they have been given is because they are not limited to the will of those special prophets who guide men to God. If miracles were the property only of those great personages, they would be more important.

Christ warned us of those false prophets who "shall show great signs and wonders, insomuch that, if it were possible, they shall deceive the very elect" (Matthew 24:24). This scripture should convince us that the ability to perform a miracle is not proof that one is a prophet of God. In fact, he could be the anti-Christ, misguiding those who are impressed by miracles.

I am not completely disdainful of miracles, however. Daily I thank God for the miracle of life, for the miracles of His life-giving Holy Spirit which has awakened me to the knowledge of my Heavenly Father, and for the miracle of the rising sun each day, bringing me physical light as well as spiritual light.

The Greatest Miracles

Alcohol and drugs can make human beings do outlandish things, but they aren't the only incentives for foolishness. Religion sometimes brings on unwise actions when its teachings are taken literally. A news item about a religious sect in England told how two of its members drowned because they tried to emulate Jesus by walking on water. The body of another member of the sect, who died of natural causes, was kept in a house for two days while other members waited for her to be lifted up to heaven.

Jesus came to teach us to perform miracles, but walking on water wasn't one of them. He wanted us mortals to live as brothers, to love one another, and to bring peace to the world. These are the greatest of miracles, and they are possible of achievement. He said so himself.

Taking the spiritual lessons of the Bible literally brings only confusion. In Isaiah 11:6 we are told that the wolf shall dwell with the lamb and the leopard shall lie down with the kid. If this passage literally refers to animals there would be no improvement in the human world. However, if it means symbolically the uniting in love of men of the nature of the mentioned animals—the vicious and the domesticated—it makes sense to me. An example of such a miracle is the conversion of Saul of Tarsus into St. Paul, enabling that "wolf" to dwell with the Lamb, Jesus Christ.

By the same token, how would the world be transformed from its present distress if everyone could walk on water, yet continue to kill his fellowmen? Not one iota!

As for the "miracle" of having a dead body raised to heaven—that incorruptible seat of eternity—the Bible tells us that the corruptible cannot become incorruptible. "Now this I say, brethren, that flesh and blood cannot inherit the kingdom of God; neither doth corruption inherit incorruption" (I Corinthians 15:50). It is the spiritual body (the soul), not the natural body that is raised to heaven. The natural body may be likened to a bird cage, the soul to the bird. When the cage is broken (the death of the body) the bird remains unharmed. In fact, it is able to soar to heaven, free at last!

The Station of Christ

Is Jesus God?

I am ever at odds with the belief that Jesus is God. I have offered many scriptures which corroborate my belief that he was not. One reason is that the word "Christ" means the "anointed." Being anointed by God places Jesus on a very high level, however, that in itself does not make him God. The fact that he was anointed shows that there is a higher source than himself. After all, the anointer is greater than the anointed. One cannot be God if there is one higher than oneself. God is the Anointer, and He is the greatest!

I accept Jesus, not as God, but as a symbol of God. His station on earth was that of God's mediator between God and mankind. A mediator is the instrument that brings two entities into relationship with one another. For instance, if one wishes to converse with someone far away, the telephone would be the mediator that brings them together. If one wishes to go to another city or country, an airplane could be the mediator between oneself and the destination one desires.

God is too far above us (not literally!) for us to come in contact with Him, so He sends us in each age a mediator to bring His Message to mankind. In one sense, the mediator (in this

this case, Jesus) could be considered God, because he is the mouthpiece of God, and although it is Jesus speaking, it is the words of God that mankind hears.

Another way to consider the matter is to see Jesus as a reflection of God—a mirror in which mankind can see God shining. If we see the sun in a mirror we might say, "There is the sun." Actually, we would be seeing the reflection of the sun. If we had two mirrors, we would see two suns, although there is only one real sun. We wouldn't be fooled by being told there were two suns. Jesus was a perfect reflection, a perfect mediator, of the attributes of God, but not of the essence of God. That alone belongs to the Most High.

Another point on this subject is that Jesus is accepted as the Son of God. It is beyond me how he, or anyone else, can be both a son and his own father.

Two Stations of Christ

One aspect of the Bible that intrigues me concerns what I call the two stations of Jesus the Christ: the human Jesus and the Christ Spirit that radiated through him.

On occasion I have pointed out scriptures that distinctly reveal these two stations. One example can be seen in his words: "I am the way, the truth and the life" (John 14:6) indicating that this was the Christ Spirit speaking through the human Jesus. On the other hand, he said, "Why callest thou me good? There is none good but one, that is, God" (Matthew 19:17). Here the human Jesus is speaking.

Another example of the two stations is revealed when he calls himself God's "only begotten Son" (John 3:16). Here the Christ Spirit is speaking. The other side of the coin, the human Jesus, is seen when he refers to himself as "the Son of man" (26 times in the Book of Matthew alone, including his references to his return).

Now, who is the Christ and how does he differ from the human Jesus? Here is what I found that made the difference crystal clear to me. The first chapter of the Gospel of John speaks of the Word that was from the beginning (1:1) and the Word was made flesh (1:14) and the Word made flesh was "the only begotten of the Father." This is the Christ Spirit that shone through the human Jesus. The human Jesus was born nearly 2,000 years ago, long after the Word (which was "from the beginning") existed. He was called the son of Abraham (Matthew 1:1). Yet, Jesus said, "Verily, verily, I say unto you, Before Abraham was, I am" (John 8:58). Here the difference between the Christ Spirit and the human Jesus is self-evident.

The Son of Man

On several occasions I have made a distinction between Jesus the man and Christ, the Holy Spirit. I believe that the human Jesus was not literally the Son of God, but it was the Christ Spirit that was honored with this rank. Jesus was born of the womb of Mary, but the Christ Spirit came from heaven. "That which is conceived in her is of the Holy Ghost" (Matthew 1:20). This scripture could not refer to the flesh and blood of Jesus because "God is a Spirit" (John 4:24) and flesh and blood cannot enter the kingdom of God (I Corinthians 15:50). This distinction is further clarified when Jesus asks his disciples, "Whom do men say that I the Son of man am?" Simon Peter said, "Thou art the Christ, the Son of the living God" (Matthew 16:13 and 16).

To me this scripture reveals that it is the Christ Spirit within him, not the physical Jesus, that represents the Son of God. On the other hand, it is his numerous references to himself as the Son of man that disclose his human station.

Here is how Jesus emphasizes his station as the Son of man in the Book of Matthew: he came to minister to the world (20:28); he came to save "that which was lost" (the lost sheep of Israel, 18:11); he declared his powers to forgive sins (9:6); and he sowed the good seed (13:37). He had no place to lay his head (8:20); he was to suffer (17:12); he was to be betrayed (17:22, 20:18, 26:2, 24, 45). He would rise from the dead (17:9); and he would return (10:23, 16:27-28, 19:28, 24:27, 30, 37, 39, 44, 25:13, 31 and 26:64).

All these references to Jesus as the Son of man reaffirm God's methôd of guiding humanity. God raises up special human beings in every age, endowing them with the Christ or Holy Spirit. I do not expect the return of the human Jesus. Instead, I believe it will be the Christ Spirit embodied in another human being.

Two Stations of the Prophets

One of the things that helped me to better understand the Bible was the knowledge that those Teachers of God who brought the great religions into being had two stations—the station of God's mouthpiece and the station of humanity. In the station of God's mouthpiece they were the recipients of the Holy Spirit, and their words were the words of God. In the station of humanity they were like all humans—they had to eat and sleep.

There are many examples in the Bible explaining what I mean. Jesus, as the mouthpiece of God, said, "I am the way, the truth and the life" (John 14:6). Then speaking as Jesus, the Son of man, he said, "Why callest thou me good? There is none good but one, that is, God" (Matthew 19:17). Again, he said, "I and my Father are one" (John 10:30), and in contrast said, "He that believeth on me, believeth not on me, but on him that sent me" (John 12:44).

Still further, he said, "Verily, verily, I say unto you, before Abraham was, I Am" (John 8:58). Contrast these words with those in Matthew 1:16, where he is depicted as a descendent of Abraham. He who was "before Abraham" represents the manifestation of the Christ or Holy Spirit—the Word that was from the beginning, as recorded in John 1:1. On the other hand, Jesus, who was a descendent of Abraham was of flesh and blood.

Another example illustrating this distinction can be seen in the passing of Muhammad. One of his followers declared, "Let him then know, whoso worshippeth Muhammad, that Muhammad is dead; but whoso worshippeth God, let him know that the Lord liveth." He was speaking of the Holy Spirit that marked Muhammad as a Teacher from God.

Jesus Was A Jew

Sometimes things said in jest turn out to be more truth than poetry. I found this to be true regarding a little poem I once heard:

> Roses are reddish,
> Violets are bluish;
> If it wasn't for Christmas,
> We'd all be Jewish.

A study of the Bible reveals that there is some truth to this meant-to-be-humorous ditty. In Matthew 15:24, Christ tells the woman of Canaan, "I am not sent but unto the lost sheep of the house of Israel." In John 4:22, he said to the woman of Samaria, "Ye worship ye know not what: we know what we worship: for salvation is of the Jews."

In Matthew 10:5-6, it is recorded that Jesus sent forth his disciples, "and commanded them, saying, Go not into the way of the Gentiles, and into any city of the Samaritans enter ye not: but go rather to the lost sheep of the house of Israel." In Luke 19:9-10, Jesus, as a guest in the house of Zacchaeus, said, "This day is salvation come to this house, forsomuch as he also is a son of Abraham. For the Son of man is come to seek and to save that which was lost."

It is quite evident from these scriptures, which the Bible presents as the words of Christ, that he did not come to start a new religion. The word "Christian" came after his crucifixion.

In addition to all of this proof of Christ's Jewishness, there is the Last Supper, in reality a Passover observance which is celebrated even today by Jews. And to complete the picture, there is an observance called the Circumcision of Christ (January 1), a Holy day in Greek, Protestant, Episcopal, Roman Catholic and other Christian churches. It celebrates Christ's observance of Jewish law.

Christ was misunderstood because he changed certain out-worn social laws, but he reiterated the Jewish spiritual laws, saying, "Think not that I am come to destroy the law, or the prophets: I am not come to destroy, but to fulfill" (Matthew 5:17). Further, he said, "For had ye believed Moses, ye would have believed me" (John 5:46).

So . . . where do we stand now? This is how I see it:

> From the scriptures of old,
> Here's a thought that's newish;
> If you believe in Christ,
> You must be Jewish.

The Prince of Peace

I have often heard Jesus referred to as being the "Prince of Peace," based presumably on the scripture in Isaiah 9:6. However, the condition of the world in his day, plus his own words, made me doubt that this title fit him. He said, "Think not that I am come to send peace on earth: I came not to send peace, but a sword" (Matthew 10:34). Also, "Suppose ye I am come to give peace on earth? I tell you, Nay; but rather division" (Luke 12:51). His prophecies in Matthew 24 carry the same theme. How, then, can he be the "Prince of Peace"?

I believe that Isaiah's prophecy refers to the "time of the end" when the Christ Spirit returns as the "Spirit of Truth" to guide mankind into all truth (John 16:13). For instance, Isaiah says that "the government shall be on his shoulder." Christ denied that, saying, "Render therefore unto Caesar the things which are Caesar's" (Matthew 22:21), thereby placing worldly government on human shoulders.

The Bible also gives clues as to Christ's station on his return. "For the Son of man shall come in the glory of his Father" (Matthew 16:27). Revelation 1:13 speaks of "one like unto the Son of man," and in 1:14, describes him as a fatherly figure. "His head and his hairs were white like wool, as white as snow."

Furthermore, in the parable of the vineyard (Matthew 21:33-41), the Lord (Father) is to come and punish the husbandmen for killing His Son. Now, since God does not come down to earth, it seems to me that the "Father" must refer to the station of the Christ on his return. The description in Revelation 1:14 fits that station. Another bit of evidence can be seen in Revelation

3:12, which promises a new name for him.

All of this indicates that the "Son of man" will come in the flesh, as a father figure, bringing once more the Christ Spirit ("Spirit of Truth") to earth. So, the Son of man is the "Prince of Peace," but in his "second coming" as a different individual.

The Shroud of Turin

The Shroud of Turin, believed by many to be the shroud of Jesus, has been called a "medieval fake" by scientists. They claim that it was made in the fourteenth century, long after Jesus died.

This comes as no surprise to me. In fact, I never could accept it as the shroud of Jesus, because no one really knows what Jesus looked like. The facial image on the shroud looks like what some artists have pictured him, but these paintings were not based on any authentic pictures, because there were none. Each artist used his own imagination in his picture of Jesus. In this country he looks like a typical gentile (non-Jew). I saw a picture of him in Haiti, drawn by a Haitian artist, in which Jesus had dark skin.

The concordance of my Bible has pictures of many of that Book's personages, but they are only figments of the minds of whoever drew them. We have no way of knowing how Moses, Jesus, the disciples, and others whose pictures appear there, looked like.

I recall a number of news items in which persons "saw" the face of Jesus. For example, one was on a screen door, another on a water tower. Publicity on such events draws crowds of people to see the phenomenon. I can understand, and I sympathize with their interest, because they are grasping for evidence of spirituality in our material world. I believe it is inherent in man to search for God, and thus they are seeking a sign of His involvement in this world.

When one "sees" Jesus on a kitchen screen or on a cloud up in the sky (from where many expect his return) or even in a dream, as some have claimed, he appears in the likeness of those pictures of him that they have seen. If he actually did appear on earth, we wouldn't recognize him because he would not fit our description of him.

As a believer in the Jewish Jesus, and as one of Jewish birth, I cannot accept as representative the various pictures of him that I have seen. It is quite possible that, instead, he appeared like what many gentiles think a typical Jew of his day looked like: perhaps having a long hooked nose and a flowing beard. His pictures portray him as being handsome, but the Bible tells us that "he hath no form nor comeliness; and when we shall see him, there is no beauty that we should desire him" (Isaiah 53:2).

False Prophets

❖❖❖❖❖❖❖❖❖❖❖❖❖❖❖❖❖❖❖❖

A True Prophet

Jesus warned us about false prophets, saying, "And many false prophets shall rise, and shall deceive many" (Matthew 24:11). How can we tell if one claiming to be a prophet is true or false? The Bible gives us many clues.

We are told, "When a prophet speaketh in the name of the Lord, if the thing follow not, nor come to pass, that is the thing which the Lord hath not spoken" (Deuteronomy 18:22). In other words, he is a false prophet.

Jesus gave us a standard by which prophets can be recognized: by their works (Matthew 7:15-20). A true prophet brings a great civilization. Moses, a lowly shepherd, took his people out of slavery and led them to the "promised land," where they became a great nation. When that civilization faltered by turning from God, then came the dispensation of Jesus, who founded the great Christian civilization.

Another true prophet whose works brought forth goodly fruits was Muhammad. A lowly camel driver, he brought unity to a divisive and barbarous people, creating an outstanding civilization. His followers fostered knowledge and science, leading in many fields, such as medicine, education, chemistry, and navigation, among others, at a time when Europe was in its dark age. Moreover, Muhammad taught his followers to revere both Moses and Jesus, telling them that their Books, the Torah and the New Testament, were true books. In fact, members of Sunni Islam expect the return of Christ in fulfillment of New Testament prophecies.

So far, men do not agree on the unity of religion, but it can be seen that the true prophets of God are unified.

With so many so-called religions popping up all around us we should scrutinize each one to separate the false from the true. St. Paul tells us to "try the spirits whether they are of God" (I John 4:1).

A true religion, like those of the past, will have its own writings, its own calendar, and, at least in its earlier years, its own martyrs. Its writings will refer to the previous religions, and tell of the next one to come. Also, it will bring new social laws to fit the age in which it comes. Its spiritual and moral teachings will be a renewal of the earlier ones, because such teachings are eternal.

Such a religion usually has its forerunner or herald, as was John the Baptist for Jesus. The Jews expected Elijah, who was to come before the Lord, and Jesus affirmed that John was Elijah in the sense that his task was the same as Elijah's.

The founder of a true religion does not force his teachings on the people to whom he is sent. He does not try to control their minds or force them to go out into the streets to make money for him. He does not ask them to live in communes or turn over all of their assets to him. He does not tell his young followers to despise their parents. He desires that his followers develop their minds to achieve the potential God has given them, and he encourages them to strive to become the image of God that is latent within them.

A true prophet covenants with his followers to love one another and to avoid prejudice of all kinds. He desires that they may become as one soul in many bodies. He is humble and desires nothing from his flock but love for each other and for

God, whom he represents on earth. He does not attract attention to himself as a person, but instead admonishes the people to acknowledge and obey the Word of God which he brings.

It is one such as this that Jesus promised, telling us to be ready, "for in such an hour as ye think not the Son of man cometh" (Matthew 24:44). That is why, in this day, "the time of the end," it is necessary to know the true prophet from the false.

"Looking For A False Messiah"

A prominent columnist once wrote on "Looking for a False Messiah." It drew my interest, since, as many clergymen believe, we are in "the last days," when Christ is to return. The columnist stated that we are seeking a false Messiah, one "who will justify our ways," instead of looking for a Messiah who "rebukes his people, shows them their errors, makes them want to be better, not stronger and richer, and asks them to make sacrifices for the common good and for the good of their own souls."

Even if we are looking for a true Messiah, we are at a disadvantage because we have a tendency to build up preconceived ideas about how he will look, where he will come from, and what he will say. This is what happened at the time of Christ's appearance nearly two thousand years ago. We confuse the symbolism of the scriptures with literal interpretations, so that when he comes, he is recognized by only a few (the "elect") who are spiritually aware, but not by the majority. The "elect" are the ones for whom the days of tribulation, as vividly portrayed in Matthew, chapter 24, shall be shortened. They are symbolized by the five wise virgins who "took oil in their vessels with their lamps" (Matthew 25:4). They had the oil of spiritual awakening, enabling them to recognize the signs of the bridegroom (the Messiah).

The difference between a true and false Messiah can be determined by their demands. If he indulges himself in material wealth while asking his followers to give it up, he is a false messiah. If he speaks in the name of the Lord, and "if the thing follow not, nor come to pass," he is a false messiah. If instead, he asks us to change our character completely and teaches us to love all mankind, we will make no mistake in following him, no matter how difficult the path.

Oneness of Religion

The "One Fold" of Christ

"And other sheep I have, which are not of this fold: them also I must bring, and they shall hear my voice; and there shall be one fold, and one shepherd" (John 10:16).

Many scoff at this belief, saying that it is impossible to bring all people into one fold or religion. The truth is that mankind is now, and always has been, of one religion. We all worship the same God, who has revealed Himself at various times to various peoples: to the Hindus through Krishna; to the Buddhists through Buddha; to the Jews through Moses; to the Christians through Jesus; to the Muslims through Muhammad, and to others at different times. Each of these Teachers brought a message befitting the age in which he appeared, and prepared his followers for the Teacher who came after him, just as a teacher in school prepares his students for the next grade.

One might ask, "If this is true, why haven't people recognized each succeeding teacher and accepted his teachings"? A study of the history of religion will show that his followers love their own prophet so much, that they become convinced that he possesses some special authority not possessed by the others.

Also, they endow him with a station of finality, despite his words to the contrary. This is why, when the next teacher does appear, with a new name, but with the same God-given Spirit, he is rejected, persecuted, and sometimes put to death as a false prophet. This can be seen in the treatment of Jesus and later Muhammad, who claimed that no prophet had suffered as he did. Today, however, multitudes worship God through both of them. Such is the agony and the ecstasy of God's prophets.

With such misunderstanding of our prophets, how can we become as one fold? The shrinking of our world through modern technology is bringing us closer together, making it imperative for us to seek the similarities in man's creeds, instead of concentrating on the differences. Already the various religions are communicating, with priests, ministers, and rabbis meeting together, leading the way to greater harmony. This couldn't have happened in earlier centuries. We are in the age of fulfillment. The Spirit of Truth is guiding us into all truth. That truth is the knowledge of humanity's oneness under the Fatherhood of God.

Jesus said that mankind would eventually become one fold. As we look around the world, this glorious goal appears to be an impossible mission. Oppressive dictators cause extreme suffering among their own and other peoples. Economic inequalities blight even our own country. It seems to be a dog-eat-dog world, where a few accumulate vast fortunes, legally and illegally (but rarely, if ever, ethically), while so many others suffer for lack of food and shelter. So, how is it possible that we will become as one fold? Our various religious beliefs separate us. If we who believe in God refuse to unite, how can we expect those who have no belief to do so?

It seems to me that the first step toward the one fold calls for unity in religion. My personal study has revealed that there are two basic differences in the various religions: the varying social laws given by God's prophets for people living in different ages under different cultures, and conflicting rituals and dogmas injected by the leaders or self-appointed spokesmen for the various religions and sects.

The spiritual or moral laws given by God are the same in

every age, but expressed in different words. All true religions teach mankind to love one another, to treat others with justice and honesty, and each in its own way brought a form of the Golden Rule. All of God's Teachers came to fulfill His laws, not to destroy them. Despite this, separation has caused religions to split into sects, and caused religions to deny the truths of other religions.

Muhammad was rejected by the followers of other religions. This was in error, according to the words of Paul, who said that "Every spirit that confesseth that Jesus Christ is come in the flesh is of God" (I John 4:2). Muhammad did confess that Christ was a true prophet from God.

We cannot truthfully judge religions by the practices of their adherents. We must judge them by the pristine teachings of their founders. When mankind realizes this, the believers of all the religions will be united under God, who is the one shepherd. When we reach that state, the world will become a new world, "a new heaven and a new earth" (Revelation 21:1).

The Oneness of Religion

I visualize the history of religion as being a mystery story in which the various chapters (revelations) outwardly appear to be unrelated. It is a mystery story because followers of each religion concentrate on their own particular chapter of God's eternal Book, ignoring the others. When mankind in general investigates all of this Book's chapters: the Hindu, Buddhist, Zoroastrian, and Islamic, as well as the Judaic and Christian (with which we of the Western world are better acquainted), people will discover that these chapters are related to each other as successive revelations of the one religion of God.

Through this discovery the "all truth," to which the Spirit of Truth is to guide us (John 16:13) will be revealed, for each revelator mentions those who came before him, and speaks of one who will come after him. When we meditate on the oneness of God, the unity or oneness of religion becomes evident. The mission of religion is to unify mankind. Thus, to say that the various religions are in competition with each other is to say that God is in competition with Himself.

The unity of religion becomes obvious to those who study the various revelations with an open mind. They will discover the same truths in each one. These revelations differ only in their social laws, which change according to the age in which each is manifested on earth.

Seeing men worship God in various temples built of stone— some in churches, some in synagogues, and others in mosques— I used to believe there were many religions. This belief disturbed me for two reasons: one, because I realized that all men were the children of one Heavenly Father, and therefore there should be only one religion; two, because I saw barriers between men, caused by the many forms of worship, in which some disputed as to which was the "right way" to worship our Glorious Creator.

To lessen my anguish, I compromised by rationalizing that in reality each person was expressing religion according to his or her own consciousness, and that the Lord heard all of His children as they worshiped Him in many languages throughout the world. With age and meditation it struck me that the various forms of worship—the rituals and dogmas—are not the sub-stance of true faith, and that true worship of God is through love for all mankind and desire to live in unity with others. These, I believe, are the works which justify one's faith.

Rituals and dogmas suffice only if man is inspired by them to fulfill the works: to love one another as Christ loves us. However, if we cling to them and fail to live the life, we fall, as Paul tells us in Romans 2:25: "For circumcision verily profiteth, if thou keep the law: but if thou be a breaker of the law, thy circumcision is made uncircumcision."

In times past, when countries appeared to be much farther apart because travel and communications were limited, such worship was, no doubt, acceptable, but in this century when our world has shrunk into a neighborhood, it is no longer tenable. The barriers raised by rituals and dogmas will eventually fade away, for these are manmade objects, and only God-revealed truths can stand the test of time.

The removal of manmade rituals and dogmas will lead us to the one true religion, fulfilling the beloved Jesus' prophecy of the one fold and the one shepherd. This God-revealed truth he brought will surely stand the test of time, for, as he said, "Heaven and earth shall pass away, but my words shall not pass away" (Matthew 24:35).

The Reflection in the Mirrors

At one time I found it extremely difficult to understand the differences in the various religions. Being a believer in one God, and recognizing the fact that mankind is one, the variations in worship, which often cause animosity and antagonism amongst religionists, was beyond my understanding. Even at this late date, with so much bloodshed in the name of religion (as we see in Northern Ireland and in Iran), I cannot see why such conditions should prevail among those who claim that they worship God.

This is how I see the differences in religion: I picture a field in which there are a number of mirrors. The sun is shining and its reflection can be seen in each mirror. Groups of people are standing in front of each mirror, worshipping the reflection of the sun in the mirror they face. Each group believes that its reflection of the sun is the only true one, swearing their allegiance to it, at the same time looking with disdain at those worshipping the reflection of the sun in the other mirrors.

Each of the mirrors represents a religion. Let us say that one religion calls its reflection of the sun Moses. Others call their reflection Jesus, Muhammad, or Buddha, etc. The misunderstanding between the various groups (or religions) comes from failing to realize that each and every one is worshipping a reflection of the same sun in a different mirror. Using the sun as a physical symbol of the spiritual Sun (God), it can be seen that all of His Reflections, such as are mentioned above, are really one in spirit (the Holy Spirit), since they are all reflections of Him, although shining forth in a different mirror, or human body.

When the followers of the various religions see that, in reality, we are all worshipping God through different reflections of Him, there will be respect, accord, and peace among them.

Progressive Revelation

One expression I often use in discussions on religion is "progressive revelation." It describes my belief that in every age God sends a Teacher to help mankind progress in spiritual knowledge even as a school teacher helps children to progress in material knowledge, at the same time preparing them for another teacher in the next grade.

I am not alone in my belief in progressive revelation. Arnold Toynbee, the famous historian, envisioned a society based on the teachings of all the great prophets of the past, from Krishna to Muhammad, and he spoke of teachings that "seers yet unborn" would bring.

Ralph Waldo Emerson was another who sensed the existence of progressive revelation. He wrote, "We are born too late for the old and too early for the new faith." He was expecting new teachings from God. He wrote that when many biblical scholars were expecting, through their interpretations of the prophecies of Daniel, the return of Christ in 1843-44.

Emerson was ridiculed by many of his day. One of his critics was John Quincy Adams, our sixth president, who said scornfully that Emerson "declares all the old revelations superannuated and worn out, and announces the approach of new revelations and prophecies." Hmm . . . wasn't that the opinion of the Pharisees, the learned in the day of Jesus? Today we know that they were wrong.

More recently (in the 1970s) a spokesman for the Koinonians, a Christian fellowship in Americaus, Georgia, stated, "We want to find out exactly what Christ is telling us today. We believe in a progressive revelation as time goes by and conditions change."

All the prophets from Krishna to Muhammad spoke of messengers of God "yet unborn" who would bring greater teachings in the days beyond their own. For example, Jesus was a future messenger of God of whom Moses spoke, and "the Spirit of Truth" is the messenger of God promised by Jesus for this day. Thus, had the followers of the great prophets also accepted the later ones, there would have been no blood shed in the name of religion, and the evils of racial and religious prejudice would never have happened. In other words, we would have possessed the kingdom of heaven on earth long, long ago.

I have occasionally written of my belief that there is only one religion and one people, created by the one God. The Holy Scriptures reveal this to be true.

The founders of each religion (in reality each revelation of the one religion of God) foretell of the next one to come. The tribe in which Jesus was born is described in Micah 5:2. In the Book of Ruth (4:1) we find that Boaz, from whom Jesus was a direct descendent, was of that tribe.

Muhammad, who accepted Moses and Jesus as true prophets of God, said, "As for me, my Lord hath guided me into a straight path; a true religion, the creed of Abraham, the sound in faith; for he was not of those who join gods with God" (Súra 6:162). Judaism and Christianity are also outgrowths of the creed of Abraham.

In Genesis 17:6, we see that God promised to make great nations out of Abraham. In 17:20, Ishmael, Abraham's son, received the promise of fathering a great nation, begetting twelve princes. It is interesting to note that Shí'ah Islam had twelve successive Imáms who reigned after Muhammad's passing. Tradition says that the twelfth Imám disappeared and is expected to return and reveal himself at "the time of the end."

Muhammad alluded to other prophets who were to come when he asked: "In what other revelation after this will they believe?" (Súra 77:50) Some students of Islam affirm that the following verse, and others of like nature, is, in reality, an allegorical prediction of two prophets to appear after Muhammad to usher in God's great Day of Judgment: "And there shall be a blast on the trumpet, and all who are in the Heavens and all who are in the earth shall expire, save those whom God shall vouchsafe to live. Then shall there be another blast on it, and lo! arising they shall gaze around them: And the earth shall shine with the light of her Lord" (39:68-69). Muslims, however, hold that no prophets will come after Muhammad.

Most people react to a new revelation by saying that its prophet has gathered the good parts of previous religions in order to proclaim himself as God's Teacher for his day. Actually, he has only renewed the spiritual laws which never change, being eternal, but which have become distorted or discarded by the people. Muhammad explained these eternal laws, saying, "Nothing hath been said to thee which hath not been said of old to apostles (prophets) before thee" (Súra 41:43).

Religion, which originated as one, must return to being one, making full circle, becoming the promised one fold (John 10:16).

Religious Prejudice Retards the Oneness of Religion

Religious prejudice exists because followers of one religion look upon followers of other religions as being in error. Christians look down on Jews, the followers of Moses, because they do not accept Jesus. Muslims look down on Christians because they do not accept Muhammad.

God sent Teachers, such as the above mentioned ones, to certain peoples in different times, each bringing the same spiritual truths and changing only the social laws to fit the age in which they appeared. The fact that each one fostered a great civilization is proof that they were sent by God. Each made such a claim.

All having been sent by God, they must be equal in station. The outward differences between them are only signs of the age in which they came. Because some seemed to have more power than others does not mean that they were superior to the rest. I believe that each of them had all knowledge, but could reveal only that which the people of that particular time could accept. Jesus had more to tell, but he knew mankind could not bear more, and he told them that the Spirit of Truth would come and guide them to all truth (John 16:12-13).

Despite the limited amount of knowledge their followers could accept, these great prophets suffered for what they did reveal. Jesus was persecuted and crucified. Muhammad said that no other prophet had suffered as he did. Yet, the messages they brought (the seeds) in time brought forth wonderful fruit. See how Christianity and Islam prospered despite their lowly beginnings.

I am assured that God sent the world Moses, Jesus, and Muhammad, among others. If this is true, then if one accepts only one prophet and rejects the others, he is rejecting God Himself, because each brought the Word of God, and the Word of God is truth.

Emerson said, "In the matter of religion, men eagerly fasten their eyes on the differences between their own creed and yours, whilst the charm of the study is in finding the agreements and identities in all the religions of men." When mankind finds the similarities in all religions, religious prejudice will no longer exist.

The Unity of the Prophets

Although He is worshipped in many different ways, nearly everyone will agree that there is only one Creator, whether He is called God, Alláh, or Jehovah. What people do not agree on is that the founders of the various known religions are, in reality, one in purpose.

Followers of each religion revere their own founder above all others, yet each founder came from the same Source, God. It makes sense to me that God has sent a different human being as His Teacher in each age, even as a school provides a different teacher for each succeeding grade. The founder of a religion 5,000 years ago could not reveal certain truths that are known today. Human beings develop from age to age, and must progress through new teachings.

In my study of the various religions I have also found that the founder of each one foretold his "return" or the coming of another. In the Hindu religion Krishna said, "Many times I have thus appeared; many times hereafter shall I come again." Buddha spoke of the coming of a universal Buddha, and Zoroastrian scriptures describe a continual parade of teachers from God, coming at times when the true teachings would be abandoned. This is the state of the world today.

An example of the unity of these Teachers is the various oceans or seas in the world. They are given different names, but actually they are connected—in reality being one body of water. Another example is in the light that comes from lamps. Each of God's Teachers is represented by a different physical lamp, but the light of each of these Holy lamps is one and the same. Jesus said, "As long as I am in the world, I am the light of the world" (John 9:5). He also spoke of the Comforter, who would be sent by God to teach mankind all things (John 14:26), and that if Jesus did not go away, the Comforter would not come (John 16:7). To me, this scripture says that the physical lamp, Jesus, who was the light of the world when on earth, promised mankind another physical lamp (the Comforter) who would bring the world more light, and the Spirit of truth, who would guide us into all truth.

The Oneness of Religion in the Qur'án

I have made some interesting discoveries in my study of Islam. Although orthodox Muslims don't believe that future prophets can appear after Muhammad, based on their literal understanding of the verse which refers to Muhammad as the "seal of the prophets" (Súra 33:40), they do accept the concept of the oneness of religion. Here are some examples: "Every nation hath had its apostle" (10:48). "And to every people have we sent an apostle saying: Worship ye God and turn away from Taghout" (16:38).* Referring to Moses, he said: "But before the Qur'án was the Book of Moses, a rule and a mercy; and this Book confirmeth it in the Arabic tongue" (46:12). Again, "And of old sent we Noah and Abraham, and on their seed conferred the gift of prophecy, and the Book. . . . Then we caused our apostles to

---

* Taghout was an Arabian idol.

follow in their footsteps; and we caused Jesus the son of Mary to follow them; and we gave him the Evangel, and we put into the hearts of those who followed him kindness and compassion" (57:26-27). "We make no distinction between any of His apostles" (2:285).

As far back as the time of Abraham, God made a covenant with mankind promising never to leave His children without the benefit of divine guidance. The Qur'án expresses the covenant in these terms: "O children of Adam! there shall come to you Apostles from among yourselves, rehearsing my signs to you; and whoso shall fear God and do good works, no fear shall be upon them, neither shall they be put to grief" (7:35). Historically the typical response to God's prophets has been: "We found our fathers with a religion, and in their tracks we tread.... We believe not in your message" (43:22-23).

In one chapter of the Qur'án Muhammad refers to the essential oneness of humanity and the purpose of the prophets to maintain the welfare and unity of the people: "Mankind was but one people; and God sent prophets to announce glad tidings and to warn; and He sent down with them the Book of Truth, that it might decide the disputes of men" (2:209). Thus all the prophets brought the same message of truth from God. Muhammad told his followers: "Nothing hath been said to thee which hath not been said of old to apostles before thee" (41:43). "Truly this your religion is the one religion" (23:54).

Muhammad

I enjoy browsing in used-book stores. I recall finding a gem—*The Speeches & Table-Talk of the Prophet Mohammad,* written by Stanley Lane-Poole, and published in London in 1882.

Mr. Lane-Poole described some of the traditions about the Prophet. One told of his gentleness and his fondness of children. He visited the sick, followed every bier he met, accepted the invitation of a slave to dinner, mended his own clothes, and waited on himself. When asked to curse someone, Muhammad said, "I have not been sent to curse, but to be a mercy to mankind."

Another tradition states, "He was the most faithful protector of those he protected, the sweetest and most agreeable in conversation. Those who saw him were suddenly filled with reverence; those who came near him loved him; they who described him would say, 'I have never seen his like either before or after.' "

When Muhammad was forty years old he received his call as a messenger of God. It was when he was praying and fasting on Mount Hira that he heard a voice say, "Recite!" He asked, "What shall I recite?" The voice said, "Recite in the name of thy Lord who created;—Created man from clots of blood. Recite! For thy Lord is the Beneficent! Who hath taught man what he knoweth not." At first Muhammad thought he was possessed with a devil, and he contemplated suicide. Then he heard the voice again, saying, "Thou art the Messenger of God, and I am Gabriel."

From then on for twenty years or more, the speeches that make up the Qur'án flowed out. Mr. Lane-Poole said, "It must be remembered that the speeches of the Qur'án are supposed to be the utterances of God, of whom Mohammad is only the mouthpiece."

Muhammad claimed that all the preceding prophets were inspired by God, and that they taught the same faith that he did. He said there was nothing new in his own doctrine. It was but the teaching of Abraham, Moses, Jesus, and all the prophets, and it confirmed all that was revealed before.

When I began my study of religion I believed that Muhammad was a blood-thirsty warrior whose followers were barbarians, vindicating their atrocities by facing east and praying five times a day. My study of the Qur'án proved to me that such a concept was entirely incorrect. This experience convinced me that one should make an independent investigation of one's own before condemning any group whose culture is different from one's own.

Actually, Muhammad condoned fighting only in defense of his religion (Súra 2:186), and pointed out that "There is no piety in turning your faces toward the east or the west, but he is pious who believeth in God, and the last day, and the angels, and the scriptures, and the prophets" (2:172).

Muhammad spoke many times of the true prophethood of Moses and Jesus, and of the truth of their books, the Old and New Testaments. He said, "Moreover, to Moses gave we 'the Book,' and we raised up apostles after him; and to Jesus, son of Mary, gave we clear proofs of his mission, and strengthened him by the Holy Spirit" (2:81).

Muhammad taught his followers to accept the virgin birth of Jesus, referring to Mary as she "who kept her maidenhood, and into whom we breathed of our spirit, and made her and her son a sign to all creatures" (21:91).

Muhammad's use of "we" and "our" is evidence of his connection with God. Compare it to the scripture in Genesis 1:16, in which God says, "Let us make man in our image, after our likeness." The expressions "us" and "our" do not refer to two Creators.

In our rapidly shrinking world, as we grow closer to all the peoples on earth, we need greater understanding of one another. What better way is there to learn about each other than by studying the beliefs and customs of those unlike ourselves? We may all discover, as I have done in my study of Islam, that not only have we been misled by historians and political leaders, but also misinformed by our religious leaders.

God's Light and the Lamps

The Bible is a very enlightening Book, especially where spiritual en-light-ening is concerned. Here we find that "the Lord is my light and my salvation (Psalm 27:1). God's Word is "a lamp unto my feet, and a light unto my path" (Psalm 119:105). Thus, God's Word is our spiritual light, guiding us in ways that will bring us eternal life.

How does God, an unknowable essence, shed this light on mankind? Through His Teachers: He has sent many Teachers to bring spiritual light to the world, and each has foretold of another who would follow in a future age with more of God's light. Moses told of another prophet, like him (Deuteronomy 18:15), and Jesus told of the coming of the Spirit of Truth (John 16:13).

Muhammad also called attention to a future revelation of truth (Súra 77:50).

With my highly imaginative mind, I symbolize God as being like electricity, and these great Teachers as the lamps through which His spiritual light shines forth to enlighten mankind. We know that lamps are lit by that mysterious force, electricity, enabling them to transmit light without being themselves the source of that light. In like manner, Jesus said, "He that believeth on me, believeth not on me, but on him that sent me" (John 12:44). He knew that God was the light and that he was the lamp.

Consider Moses bringing forth the Ten Commandments from God: "For the commandment is a lamp; and the law is light" (Proverb 6:23). The commandments came through Moses (the lamp) and God's law was the light. In John 8:12, Jesus states, "I am the light of the world," meaning that God's light was manifest in Jesus, who was God's Lamp. That he was the lamp and not the light can be seen by his words, "My doctrine is not mine, but his that sent me" (John 7:16).

God's Mediator is Always Rejected

Because God is an unknowable essence, He sends a Mediator in each age to bring His laws. Unfortunately, when that Mediator comes, he is rejected or persecuted, sometimes crucified before he is accepted (usually long after he is dead). Strangely enough, those who pray for his coming, especially the clergy, are the ones who treat him in that manner.

At the time of his coming the world is in a degraded state spiritually. The condition of religion is one of ritual and dogma, and its leaders have acquired power and prestige. They become the blind leading the blind. When the long-awaited one reveals himself, he comes, not as a king, but as a very humble person who exposes the shortcomings of these religious leaders, angering them.

These leaders have misinterpreted the signs of his coming, so they look upon him as a false prophet, and they begin their tragic persecution of their Lord. In addition, the Mediator from God is known in the area where he reveals himself, causing further confusion. "A prophet is not without honor, save in his own country, and in his own house" (Matthew 13:57).

In reference to this condition, P. J .A. Feuerbach wrote, " 'Can any good come out of Nazareth?' This is always the question of the wiseacres and knowing ones. But the good, the new comes exactly from that quarter whence it is not looked for, and is always something different from what is expected. Everything new is received with contempt, for it begins in obscurity. It becomes a power unobserved."

"Watch ye therefore, for ye know not when the master of the house cometh" (Mark 13:35). Who are we to watch for? For the Mediator who will come from an unexpected quarter, like "a thief in the night" (I Thessalonians 5:2).

Unity in Religion Necessary to Peace

Before we can have universal peace, we must have unity. Attaining unity is impossible as long as we continue to separate ourselves by our various concepts and worship of God. We may be on different paths approaching Him, but we must also consider that there must be a convergence of all religions in unity. This means becoming the one fold, foretold by Jesus, before we can have the kind of peace that will give birth to the kingdom of God on earth.

As long as each religion (and denomination) believes that it alone has all truth, universal peace cannot become a reality. The belief that when Christ returns we will automatically be unified by his appearance is wishful thinking. We on earth are the instruments through which unity will be achieved. As long as religions and denominations disagree with each other, we cannot fulfill this destiny for which we were created.

How can we become the instruments of unity? We must recognize that all the Teachers of God, including Buddha, Krishna, Zoroaster, Moses, Jesus, and Muhammad, were sent by God to bring us His words for mankind. Each was a lamp bringing

God's Light. As lamps (their human personalities), they were distinctly different. However, the Spiritual Light that shone forth from these lamps is the same.

Two Kinds of Ordinances in Religion

It is strange that although the prophet-founders of the divinely-revealed religions are conjoined in perfect unity, their followers are in strife with each other. This attitude of religious prejudice stems from man's misunderstanding of the dual purpose for which all the great prophets appeared on earth: namely, to revitalize the spiritual laws, which are eternal, and to lay down the social laws needed for the age in which each appeared.

Each religion embodies two kinds of ordinances. The first concerns spiritual truths: the development of a moral life, and the quickening of the heart, prayer and worship of God, and service and goodwill to others. These are fundamental, one and the same in all religions, changeless and eternal, not subject to transformation. These are the laws Jesus came not to destroy but to fulfill (Matthew 5:17).

The second kind of ordinance in the divinely-revealed religions is that which relates to the material or social affairs of mankind. These are laws that are subject to change in each age, according to the needs and the changing capacities of humanity. Surely, we cannot live today by the social laws of the day of Moses: "an eye for an eye." It is the changing of these laws that causes strife among followers of the various religions. When Jesus abrogated the laws of the Sabbath and divorcement, it caused consternation among the Jews.

Ironically, one of the proofs of a true prophet is the changing of these laws in each age. It is just as necessary to change the social laws as it is to renew and reaffirm the spiritual laws. By accepting the truth that all things in this temporal world must change and evolve, we will become united, thus ending strife on earth.

Religious Truth is Relative

In religion the tendency has been to accept truth as being absolute and unchanging. Truth is relative, for as man advances in knowledge, his understanding of religion develops. For instance in 1616 the Church accepted the concept that the sun revolved around the earth. When Galileo proclaimed the opposite, he was called a heretic and was imprisoned and tortured. Galileo later was proven to be right.

Actually, truth never changes, but man's understanding of it changes as his knowledge increases from age to age. Thus, in each succeeding age he gets a fuller picture of his world, just as he gets a more complete picture of a jigsaw puzzle as he places more pieces in it.

Christ, who knew all truth, spoke of its relativity and of the need for man to grow in order to grasp more knowledge of God's creation. He said, "I have yet many things to say unto you, but ye cannot bear them now" (John 16:12). He knew that man would understand his words in an age beyond his lifetime. Muhammad also affirmed the relativity of revealed truth according to the age in which it appears: "To each age its Book. What He pleaseth will God abrogate or confirm: for with Him is the Source of Revelation" (Súra 13:38, 39).

The Jewish people failed to recognize Jesus as their messiah because their religious leaders accepted truth as being absolute. They thought they knew it all, thus keeping them from recognizing truth in its larger form when Jesus appeared in their midst. He pointed out the error of their ways by saying, "For had ye believed Moses, ye would have believed me, for he wrote of me" (John 5:46). Moses had prepared his people for the greater truth brought by Jesus, but they fell into error.

Is it possible for the modern interpreters of religion to fall into the same error? Those who persecuted Galileo and other great scientists have already done so. Accepting "truth" as an absolute can prevent today's religionists from recognizing the Comforter, "even the Spirit of Truth" who shall guide us into all truth (John 16:13).

In my search for truth I have come to one conclusion, and that is that I can come to no conclusion. Sounds silly, doesn't it? Well, we human beings, seeking truth, at times feel that we have found it, only to discover that today's truth is not always the truth of tomorrow.

I feel I can best describe this by visualizing a giant picture, the picture of absolute truth, the perfect creation of God, of which we see only a small portion. When we judge that picture by the tiny portion we see, we judge wrongly. As humanity grows from age to age, it gets a greater perspective as it sees more and more of the picture. Our concepts change, and our knowledge of the picture is altered accordingly.

The truth of 2,000 years ago bound men to the surface of the earth, but today's truth finds us in space and far below the surface of the sea. A few hundred years ago, for one to deny the "truth" that the sun revolved around the earth would bring him punishment by death. Today we know that the reverse is true.

Religious Cycles

The coming of spring reminds me of cycles. One day is a cycle of twenty-four hours (one day and one night). One year is a cycle of 365 days, plus 5 hours, and 48 and a fraction minutes. There is a cycle of eclipses, a period required for the revolution of the moon's node: about 18 years and 11 days, after which eclipses usually return in a similar manner. There is also a metonic cycle: a period of 19 years which, being completed, the new and full moon returns at the same time of the year.

An interesting thing about cycles is this: the end of one cycle means the beginning of another like cycle. Thus, the end of a day means the beginning of another day; the end of a year means the beginning of another year, and so on.

The Bible speaks of cycles, too. For instance, God said to Daniel: "Shut up the words, and seal the book, even to the time of the end" (Daniel 12:4). In Hebrews, chapter 1, we are informed that God "hath in these last days spoken unto us by his Son." These "last days" signify the end of a cycle, the Mosaic cycle, marking the beginning of another: that of the Christian cycle, for the end of a cycle marks the beginning of another cycle.

Turning to the 24th chapter of Matthew, we read of another "time of the end" when Christ is to return. Jesus said, "And this gospel of the kingdom shall be preached in all the world for a witness unto all nations; and then shall the end come."

Jesus warned us to "be awake" to watch for him, the Spirit of Truth, who is to come "like a thief in the night," to bring a new cycle, this time the cycle of the kingdom of Heaven on earth. Meditation on the scriptures will reveal the true meaning of the spiritual cycles. They will then become as self-evident as the physical cycles of the earth, the sun, and the moon, which we accept through common experience as gospel truth.

Divinely revealed religions go through cycles in three stages. In the first stage the Teacher who brings a new revelation, as well as his followers, is persecuted, with many, often including the Teacher himself, being martyred for his teachings.

In the second stage, the Teacher's cause takes hold and he is revered by a growing number of followers, including some who are descendents of the original persecutors.

In the third stage of the cycle the bulk of his followers fall away from the pristine teachings he brought, giving only lip service and injecting various rituals and dogmas that were never taught.

When the falling away reaches a crucial stage; when iniquity abounds and the love of many waxes cold (Matthew 24:12), we can know that the "time of the end" is at hand. That is why Jesus gave the warning to "watch therefore: for ye know not what hour your Lord doth come" (Matthew 24:42).

Man can discern the face of the sky, but finds it difficult to discern the signs of the times (Matthew 16:3). It is at such a time that the cycle is renewed through a new Teacher, a new "Son of man." This process reminds me of a thermostat, a spiritual one, that registers the condition of love in the world. When man's love grows cold the thermostat goes into action, bringing a new Teacher, who once again regenerates love amongst mankind.

Those who cling to the outworn rituals persecute him and his followers. This is the renewal of the first cycle.

Scientists have discovered that the whole universe, from the tiny atom to the gigantic galaxies, works in uniformity, and that everything operates in cycles.

Each year has a cycle of seasons: spring, summer, autumn, and winter. These cycles never change. Religion also appears in cycles, though not as precise in times. But it does have its four seasons. When a Teacher comes from God it is the spiritual springtime. As his teachings begin to take hold, it becomes the spiritual summer, and its growth increases. Then comes the spiritual autumn when the fruits are gathered. Later, the spiritual winter sets in, when men turn away from God and religion becomes more a dead form. Love of material things takes precedence over the love of God. As things become frigid, God's thermostat goes to work through the coming of another Teacher, who brings another spiritual springtime, and the cycles begin all over.

Prophecies and Signs

The Chariots Shall Rage In The Streets

For quite a few years my mind has been focused on religion, being interested in biblical prophecy and its fulfillment. Thus, I was intrigued by the book *Exodus*, for it appeared to me, as I read it, that it was a dramatic story of the fulfillment of prophecy in the Holy Land.

I was especially impressed by the incident of the airlift of the Yemenite Jews into Israel. Those folks, still living as in ancient biblical times, holding fast to Old Testament scripture, accepted the strange "birds" which carried them to the Promised Land as a fulfillment of Isaiah 40:31, which reads, "But they that wait upon the Lord shall renew their strength; they shall mount up with wings as eagles."

I found other prophecies that seemed to foretell the future. One was about the telephone, another about the automobile. Reading from Psalm 19:4, we find, "Their line is gone out through all the earth, and their words to the end of the world." (Telephone?) I can picture the automobile, expressways, head-lights, and "hot rods" in Nahum 2:4: "The chariots shall rage in the streets, they shall jostle one against another in the broad ways; they shall seem like torches; they shall run like the lightnings."

Being convinced that the prophets of old were adept at describing our modern devices, I was not surprised when I saw an ad in *Time Magazine* (October 31, 1960) showing a giant shovel, captioned "World's biggest shovel moves mountains in minutes." It was described as follows: "Its dimensions are staggering: height, 20 stories; weight, 14 million pounds; reach, more than a city block. It will be able to pick up 173 tons of material at one bite." Recalling a particular scripture, I reached for my Bible and found what I was looking for in Isaiah 41:15. It states, "Behold, I will make thee a new sharp threshing instrument having teeth: thou shalt thresh the mountains, and beat them small, and shalt make the hills as chaff."

Well described, isn't it? No wonder I am convinced that prophecy is being fulfilled before our eyes. What do you think? Is it just coincidence or is the new day of God dawning?

The Great Earthquake

Of all the books of the Bible, the Book of Revelation is the most exciting to me because of my interest in symbolism. There is no doubt that much of that book is symbolic. For instance, the mention of "a new heaven and a new earth" (21:1). The literal heaven above us (the sky) and the earth upon which we live will always be the same ones they have been.

I have discovered, however, that some of the prophecies appear to have been fulfilled literally as well. I refer to Revelation 6:12-13. Here it is recorded (John the Divine is speaking), "And I beheld when he (the Lamb) had opened the sixth seal, and lo, there was a great earthquake; and the sun became black as sackcloth of hair, and the moon became as blood, and the stars of heaven fell unto the earth . . ."

These prophecies were to be fulfilled before the "time of the end." Many biblical scholars of the last century, using the prophecies of Daniel 8,13-14 calculated that 1844 would be the "time of the end." Therefore, it would seem, if their calculations were correct, that the three prophecies mentioned above would have to occur before (but not very much before) 1844.

Let's start with the first prophecy—that of the "great earthquake." We have had some great ones, such as that in San Francisco in 1906, but there was one that was the greatest recorded since the time of Christ. It occurred in Lisbon, Portugal on November 1, 1775.

Here is a report of that event: "At twenty minutes to ten on the morning of November 1, 1775, Lisbon was firm and magnificent, on one of the most picturesque and commanding sites in the world—a city of superb approach. In six minutes the great city was in ruins . . . half of the world felt the convulsion. In Sweden, Africa, and the West Indies . . . the perturbations were felt for more than a month afterward, even in distant parts of Europe."

Another report said, "The conflagration lasted a whole week. There was a tidal wave and floods. Six million people were affected by this great earthquake."

Coincidence? Or was this really a fulfillment of prophecy? I'll take up the other two prophecies mentioned here in future columns.

The Dark Day

Recently I wrote of three prophecies in Revelation 6:12-13 that appear to have been fulfilled literally. They were "a great earthquake," the sun becoming "black as sackcloth of hair," and the falling of stars on the earth. I described reports of the great earthquake. Today we shall find out about the "Dark Day" when the sun was completely darkened.

The historical day that became the "Dark Day" occurred in 1780. One report on this event said, "On May 19, 1780, the birds, animals, and people rose as usual and sang their morning songs. By 10 a.m., a thick darkness covered the land, and the animals again went to bed."

In the *Memoirs of the American Academy of Arts and Sciences* published in Boston in 1785, A. N. Hollis, Professor of Mathematics and Philosophy at Harvard College, wrote a lengthy article about the remarkable darkness of this "Dark Day," which lasted from 15 to 20 hours. Professor Hollis stated that the darkness was not caused by any eclipse, a fact that was proven by the relative positions of the planets of our system at that time, since the moon was more than 150 degrees from the sun on that day. There were no clouds or smoke that could cause such an extended darkness, in which even artificial light (lamps or candles) seemed to make no impression.

Webster's Unabridged Dictionary, edition 1883, gives an account of this unexplainable darkness, and ends by stating that "the true cause of this remarkable phenomenon is unknown." This was confirmed from many sources and the historical cause of the darkness has yet to be explained. The famous poet John Greenleaf Whittier wrote a poem about this event titled "The Dark Day."

The Falling Stars

I am continuing with the reports on the literal fulfillment of the prophecies in Revelation 6:12-13, regarding the great earthquake, the darkening of the sun, and the falling of the stars on earth, the topic of today's column.

This celestial display of stars (actually meteors) occurred on the nights of November 12–13, 1833, the stars breaking like a tempest over the earth, pelting North America from the Gulf of Mexico to Halifax, Canada. The French astronomer, Flammarion, wrote, "At the moment of maximum it was like half the number of snow flakes which we perceive in the air during an ordinary shower of snow, estimated at 34,000 stars an hour."

Dr. H. H. Jessup, professor at the Presbyterian College of Beirut, wrote, "On the morning of the fourteenth (of November) at three o'clock, I was aroused from a deep sleep by the voice of [a] young man, calling, 'The stars are coming down'.... The meteors poured down like a rain of fire blown by a mighty wind. ... One immense green meteor came down over Lebanon, seeming as large as the moon, and exploded with a loud noise, leaving a green pillar of light in its train. The Mohammedans gave the call to prayer from the minarets, and the common people were in terror."

Thoughtful people were awed by the fulfillment of the prophetic signs of Christ. Professor Alexander Twining, civil engineer and instructor at Yale University, writing about this phenomenon, stated, "Had they held on their course unabated for three seconds longer, half a continent must, to all appearances, have been involved in an unheard of calamity. But that Almighty Being Who made the world, and knew its dangers, gave it also its armature, endowing the atmospheric medium around it with protecting, no less-than-life supporting properties."

Noted astronomer Simon Newcomb and other scientists stated that there was no known explanation for this phenomenon.

Symbolic Meaning of Revelation 6:12-13

In several recent columns I wrote of the literal fulfillment of the prophecies in Revelation 6:12-13, referring to a great earthquake, the darkening of the sun, and the falling of stars on earth. Now I will give what I believe are the symbolic fulfillments of these same prophecies.

My source on this subject is *New Keys to the Book of Revelation*, by Ruth J. Moffett. She wrote that earthquakes symbolize the great changes that take place in human affairs at the end of a religious cycle, such as social, political, and ecclesiastical upheavals which shake the very foundation of established traditions. This happens in every age when another messenger from God appears on earth.

When Jesus came 2,000 years ago, he changed certain social laws, such as the law of divorce (Mark 10:11-12, Luke 16:18, and I Corinthians 7:10, 39). He disputed the narrow interpretation of the Sabbath rules and customs, antagonizing the Pharisees. He said, "The Sabbath was made for man, and not man for the Sabbath" (Mark 2:27).

Regarding the darkening of the sun, the symbolism refers to

people's spiritual apathy when the pure teachings of God's Word become obscured ("darkened") by misunderstanding and prejudice. Such was the case of Moses' teachings at the time of Jesus, who came to renew the religion of God. I believe that is why he said, "For had ye believed Moses, ye would have believed me: for he wrote of me" (John 5:46).

As for the stars falling on earth, even the literal fulfillment was in a sense symbolic, because they were not stars, but instead, meteors that fell. Individual stars are many times larger than the earth. One star striking the earth would destroy it. The symbolic meaning given by my source states that falling stars represent religious leaders who have become debased and worldly-minded. Thus, John the Baptist referred to the Pharisees as vipers (Matthew 3:7), and Jesus called them hypocrites (Matthew 23:27). Even today, according to news items, some clergymen have become worldly-minded, being involved in immoral activities. It's a sign of the "time of the end."

Prophecies in Matthew Chapter 24

Of all the chapters in the Bible, the 24th chapter of Matthew is, to me, the most enlightening regarding the "time of the end." That chapter is full of information, literal and symbolic, depicting the time of the return of the Christ. For instance, when his disciples asked him about the "end of the world," he said, "For many shall come in my name, saying, I am Christ; and shall deceive many" (24:5). He was warning them of false prophets. The reason for this warning is clarified by Christ's statement in Revelation 3:12, where he alludes to the fact that he will bear a new name upon his return.

Christ spoke of wars and rumors of wars, with nation against nation, and of famines, pestilences, and earthquakes. Today we read about these "signs of the end" in the newspapers. As is recorded in Matthew 24:12, the love of many has grown cold. At present hate seems to be the order of the day.

He tells us that the sun shall be darkened, the moon shall not give her light, and the stars shall fall from heaven (24:29). The symbolism here, as I see it, refers to certain reflectors of God's light—the religious leaders—who shall fail him—even as they did 2,000 years ago.

I believe that the materialistic condition of our world today, wherein many clergymen are leaving the temples and the churches, is sufficient evidence marking the dimming of the light of religion. This exodus from the houses of worship could mean the end of the need for the clergy, because the City of God will not need the sun or moon to lighten it, "for the glory of God did lighten it" (Revelation 21:23).

The bright note in the 24th chapter of Matthew is that, despite the "great tribulation, such as was not since the beginning of the world to this time" (24:21), these days will be shortened for the elect's sake. This indicates that the "end of the world" means the end of a cycle, not the total destruction of the world.

The Time of the End

Is this truly the "time of the end"? I believe that the 24th chapter of Matthew gives a number of clues to indicate that it is indeed. We have wars and threats of war (24:6). Nation is rising against nation, and there are famines, pestilences, and earthquakes in diverse places (24:7). The latest of the pestilences, AIDS, is spreading rapidly. Tremors are being recorded in California and elsewhere, and scientists are warning that more is to come.

Judging from the rise of many new religions and cults, some brainwashing young people, false prophets are deceiving many (24:11). The gospel of the Kingdom has been preached in all the world, of which it is written, "And then shall the end come" (24:14).

Many biblical scholars claimed that this has actually happened, choosing circa 1844 as the time, through their interpretations of the prophecies of Daniel. Jesus refers to Daniel concerning "the abomination of desolation" (24:15). Considering the present breakdown of family life, and the increase of pollution, pornography, crime (both street and white collar), and political dishonesty, it is quite clear to me that the desolation of our world is more abominable than in any previous age. Sure, we've always had such problems, but today's problems match Matthew 24:21, where it is written, "For then there shall be great tribulation, such as was not since the beginning of the world to this time, no, nor ever shall be."

It is my belief that the signs of the "time of the end" are being, or have been to a great extent, fulfilled. Two thousand years ago Jesus was rejected by those who did not recognize in what hour their Messiah had come. That is why, with all these signs, it is important to "watch therefore" (24:42), since those who say in their hearts, "my Lord delayeth his coming" (24:48), shall be cut asunder (24:51).

The Book of Zephaniah, short but loaded with prophecy, brings into focus the "time of the end" in which we are living. He tells us, "The great day of the Lord is near" (1:14), and that it will be "a day of wrath, a day of trouble and distress, a day of wasteness and desolation" (1:15). Sounds familiar, doesn't it? He warned those who, like those today, hoard silver and gold, saying, "Neither their silver nor their gold shall be able to deliver them in the day of the Lord's wrath" (1:18). He promised that the Israelites would be gathered and become honored people: "For I will make you a name and a praise among all people of the earth, when I turn back your captivity" (3:20). Since Israel has been gathered it is time to watch carefully (investigate all things) lest we miss our promised one. "So likewise ye, when ye shall see all these things, know that it is near, even at the doors" (Matthew 24:33).

A New Sodom and Gommorah

As our world's sicknesses—the wars, racial prejudice, crime, poverty and famine, pollution (and the rest of the ten modern plagues)—worsen, and humanity wonders what it all means, I find the answers in the Bible. As confusing as the times seem, those who are spiritually awakened recognize that even as it was nearly two thousand years ago, we are in "the last days" (Hebrews 1:2) again, and a purging process is at hand. We are living in the days described by Jesus in the 24th chapter of Matthew.

I began to realize how evil things are getting when, after a number of years, I casually glanced over the "amusement" pages of one of our daily newspapers. I was shocked to read some of the descriptions of the movies in the ads. I wouldn't dare (or want to) mention those descriptions in my column, nor the descriptions of some of the stage acts shown at "high class" hotels and night clubs.

Our cities have become like Sodom and Gommorah, whose destruction by brimstone and fire came through their sinfulness. If our cities continue in their downward direction, their fate will be the same. In II Peter 2:6, we are told that Sodom and Gommorah are examples "unto those that after should live ungodly."

The nuclear bomb is the fire and brimstone of this age, poised for its destructive, yet cleansing, purpose. Those who survive such a catastrophe, should it happen, would then clearly recognize their neglect of the unifying teachings of God.

Isaiah Sees Our Time

One of the most informative books in the Bible is the Book of Isaiah. I can associate this Book with today's happenings, as well as with prophecies that were fulfilled by Christ's appearance nearly 2,000 years ago. A classic example is the first chapter of that Book. Here he speaks of a "sinful nation, a people laden with iniquity, a seed of evildoers, children that are corrupters: they have forsaken the Lord" (1:4). The present condition of our

114 The Bible Revisited

country fairly well fits this description.

Continuing, he said, "Thy silver is become dross, thy wine mixed with water" (1:22). Just look at our "silver" coins today. As for the wine, some bars have been accused of "cutting" their products by diluting them with water. I'm sure these culprits are unaware that they are fulfilling Bible prophecy. Isaiah also said, "Thy princes are rebellious, and companions of thieves (Watergate, for example?); every one loveth gifts (political bribery?), and followeth after rewards (TV give-away shows?): they judge not the fatherless, neither doth the cause of the widow come unto them" (too little funds for human needs?) (1:23).

In the same chapter Isaiah brings signs of hope, foretelling the salvation of mankind. He speaks of the "elect," as does Matthew at a later date. He said, "Except the Lord of Hosts had left unto us a very small remnant, we should have been as Sodom, and we should have been like unto Gomorrah" (1:9). This could also refer to the return to the Holy Land of the Israelites. (This is further explained in Isaiah 10:21-22 and 11:11-12.)

Isaiah warned those who abide only by the rituals of religion because they failed to "learn to do well; seek judgment, relieve the oppressed, judge the fatherless, plead for the widow" (1:17).

The Return of Christ

🔯🔯🔯🔯🔯🔯🔯🔯🔯🔯🔯🔯🔯🔯🔯🔯🔯🔯🔯🔯🔯🔯

The Return of Christ

Unable to accept traditional concepts regarding the return of Christ, I decided to make my own independent investigation of the Bible. As a Jew, I had already accepted Jesus as my Messiah through my studies of the Old Testament (the Masoretic text that is used in the synagogues), even though it did not mention him by name. Therefore, I concluded that the New Testament would contain the evidence I was seeking.

Here are the clues that gave me a new concept of the return of Christ: speaking of the future, Jesus said, "I have yet many things to say unto you, but ye cannot bear them now. Howbeit, when he, the Spirit of Truth, is come, he will guide you into all truth" (John 16:13).

What is the "Spirit of Truth"? It is another way of saying the "Word of God," the "Holy Ghost," and the "Christ Spirit." They all signify the universal Spirit or Will that emanates from the Creator. Since Jesus said, "*he*, the Spirit of Truth," it is certain that he meant the return of that Spirit in another human being. Surely, when he said, "Before Abraham was, I am," he didn't mean that he had appeared at that earlier date as the same physical Jesus of 2,000 years ago. Another clue I found was the statement of Jesus that one cannot put new wine into old bottles, lest it break the old bottles (Mark 2:22, Matthew 9:17, and Luke 5:37). Christ lso indicated that on his return he would come bearing a new ame (Revelation 3:12).

One subject that often arises when I discuss religion with another person is the return of Christ. There seems to be two schools of thought on this matter: He has not returned but is coming, and he will not return in the flesh because his spirit is with us always.

I question both opinions. I do believe in his coming, but I also believe he has come several times. He said, "Before Abraham was, I am" (John 8:58). He also said he would "come quickly" (Revelation 22:7, 12, 20). I feel sure that "quickly" means sooner than 2,000 years, especially since the Bible tells us that each day with the Lord is as a thousand years (II Peter 3:8). I understand the Lord's day as being each age in which He sends the Holy Spirit in human form. Christ came in "these last days" (Hebrews 1:2). The "last days" of one cycle mark the beginning of a new Day of God.

The belief that Christ won't return in the flesh is refuted several times in the Bible. When his disciples asked him about the return, he spoke of that return as the "coming of the Son of man" (Matthew 24:27). He also said, "Ye shall not see me henceforth, till ye shall say, Blessed is he that cometh in the name of the Lord" (Matthew 23:39).

Biblical scholars of the last century, studying the Book of Daniel, concluded that Christ would return in 1843 or 1844. Because no one, even the Seventh Day Adventists, who put so much emphasis on the year 1844, recognized anyone coming with the Christ Spirit, many gave up on the idea of his return in the flesh. However, we must remember that the people of two thousand years ago also failed to recognize "the signs of the times," and since history repeats itself, it is possible that the Christ, coming once more in human form as the Spirit of Truth, may have come and gone.

Perhaps the greatest glory a believer in Christ can imagine is being on earth at his return. Those who look forward to it, believe they will recognize him, because he is to come "in the clouds of heaven with power and great glory" (Matthew 24:30). Unfortunately, many take this scripture literally, a fallacy, in my mind.

In meditating on the return, my mind goes back nearly 2,000 years ago. Only a few people recognized Jesus as their Messiah. I wondered why. It should have been easy to recognize him then, but he came from a place they knew: Nazareth, a town held in contempt. "Can there any good thing come out of Nazareth?" (John 1:46). Furthermore, he changed certain social laws, forbidding divorce (Mark 10:11-12) and broadening the meaning of the Sabbath, which the Pharisees interpreted narrowly. He said, "The Sabbath was made for man, and not man for the Sabbath" (Mark 2:27).

These facts made it very difficult for the people of his day to recognize him, especially since their religious leaders condemned him. These changes were "clouds" which hid the Spiritual Sun from shining through. Such "clouds" are tests sent by God as a warning to men to "watch therefore" (Matthew 24:42). If Christ is to be easily recognized on his return, such a warning would not have been necessary.

As I see it, the "clouds of heaven" in which Christ is to return are spiritual clouds which darken the hearts of those who "seeing, see not; and hearing they hear not, neither do they understand" (Matthew 13:13). If Christ's first coming is any guide to his second appearance, only a few will recognize him on his return. After all, he said he came down from heaven the first time, and no one recognized him then (John 3:13).

In the Glory of the Father

Despite the belief of many, I doubt that men could recognize Christ upon his return, as they expect. Even if he looked as he did 2,000 years ago he would be hard to recognize because we really don't know exactly how he looked.

I believe his coming is to be, not as the Son of God, but in the station of the "Father," a spiritual station representing God Himself even as Jesus represented the spiritual station of the "Son." Revelation 1:13–14 refers to one like the Son of man, and describes him thus: "His head and his hairs were white like wool, as white as snow..." This is a symbol of a fatherly figure. Further, Matthew 16:27 tells us that "the Son of man shall come in the glory of his Father."

I found more evidence in the Parable of the Vineyard (Matthew 21:33-41). Here Jesus spoke of a certain landowner who planted a vineyard and let it out to husbandmen before going on a long journey. When the fruit was nearly ready, he sent servants to receive the fruits. However, the husbandmen beat, stoned, and even killed the servants. Then the landowner sent his son, whom they also killed. The parable ends with the prospect of the landowner himself coming to the vineyard to punish the husbandmen for their evil deeds. The landowner is God, the husbandmen are the leaders of the people, the servants are His prophets, and the son is Jesus, who was crucified. Finally, God, who is a Spirit, incorruptible in essence (John 4:24), will manifest the Christ Spirit in a chosen human individual as the "Father" ("hairs white as snow")—as the Comforter, or the Spirit of Truth" —and He will "punish them for their ways" (Hosea 4:9).

As A Thief In The Night

A local newspaper reported the opinions of four clergymen on the return of Christ, which, according to Reverend Billy Graham, is "imminent." All four agreed on this point, but differed on how, when, and where the return would take place. I am not surprised that people are confused about religious matters when their spiritual leaders cannot agree on such important subjects as the return of Christ.

Although the Bible states that no one knows the exact hour when the return will take place, many believe they will recognize him when he comes. Jesus knew that only a few, the "elect," would recognize him. That is why he warned people to "Watch therefore: for ye know not what hour your Lord doth come. But know this, that if the goodman of the house had known in what watch the thief would come, he would have watched, and would not have suffered his house to be broken up" (Matthew 24:42-43).

Who is the goodman and who is the thief? It appears to me that the goodman is a spiritual person, perhaps a religious leader, a teacher of righteousness. The thief is Christ himself: "for yourselves know perfectly that the day of the Lord so cometh as a thief in the night" (I Thessalonians 5:2).

Nearly two thousand years ago, the religious leaders of Judaism momentarily expected their Messiah, and knew him not when he came, because outwardly he did not fulfill their literal interpretations. See, then, how their house was "broken up" when Christ came "as a thief in the night." Can it be that today's religious leaders are doing likewise? It is almost 2,000 years since Christ said, "Behold, I come quickly" (Revelation 3:11 and 22:7), and "Surely, I come quickly" (22:20).

Biblical scholars of the last century, using the prophecy of Daniel (8:14) concluded that the return was to be in 1843 or 1844. Can it be that, once again, the literal interpretations of today's religious leaders, who are expecting the return momentarily, have missed him?

Christ promised us that he would return and he gave us many signs by which we can recognize him. Although it is true that he said that no one except his Father knew the day or the hour of his return, he repeatedly admonished the people to be watchful: "Watch therefore: for ye know not what hour your Lord doth come" (Matthew 24:42). He warned them to be on guard "lest coming suddenly he find you sleeping" (Mark 13:36).

I mention these scriptures because, when I express my belief to those who come to my door to witness for their Lord, that it is possible he has already returned, they invariably say that the Bible says that no one knows the time of his return.

The Bible says much more on this subject. As I mentioned before, it warns us continually to "be awake." This I interpret as keeping the mind open for investigating anyone who claims to be the Christ returned. For instance, Paul said to "try the spirits whether they are of God" (I John 4:1).

Jesus, who came "as a thief in the night" 2,000 years ago, knew that many would fail to recognize him as they did then. Thus, he said, "O ye hypocrites, ye can discern the face of the sky; but can ye not discern the signs of the times?" (Matthew 16:3). He gave a perfect example in the parable of the virgins, five of whom failed to be prepared, lacking the oil of spirituality, causing them to miss their Lord (Matthew 25). Therefore, we must, while being aware of false prophets, keep open minds lest our fate be that of the oil-less virgins.

It is quite evident that this is the "time of the end" when all the signs of Christ's return are being fulfilled, so it should be a day of alertness for that return. It should be easy to recognize false prophets. "When a prophet speaketh in the name of the Lord, if the thing follow not, nor come to pass, that is the thing which the Lord hath not spoken, but the prophet hath spoken it presumptuously: thou shalt not be afraid of him" (Deuteronomy 18:22). The best way to know whether one is a false or true prophet is to follow Paul's advice, to "try the spirits whether they are of God."

The Return of Elijah

The prophet-founders of the great religions: Moses, Jesus, Muhammad, Krishna, Buddha, and Zoroaster wrote or spoke of future prophets who would come to extend the spiritual knowledge of mankind. Some indicated that they, themselves, would return, and others said another prophet would appear. Jesus gave reference to both.

Although many of his followers are expecting the actual return of Jesus, history tells us that up to now each succeeding prophet-founder of a religion has been a different person bringing the same message from God in an updated form to the age in which he came.

An excellent example of how the "return" can mean the coming of a different human being in the same spiritual station is seen in regard to John the Baptist. When asked if he was Elijah, who was prophesied by Malachi (4:5) to come before the Lord, he denied it (John 1:21). On the other hand, when Jesus was asked the same question, he said that in truth John was Elijah (Mark 9:13 and Matthew 17:12).

When Jesus was asked by his disciples about his return, he referred to it as the coming of "the Son of man" (Matthew 24:27, 30 and 39). He referred to the Son of man as "he," not as himself (Matthew 24:31). Jesus also referred to the return as "he the Spirit of Truth," which in no way could mean that the same physical Jesus would come to earth.

As I see it, each of the great prophets hold the same station, even as John the Baptist held the same station as Elijah. Each one was imbued with the same Holy Spirit, although they were different human beings. I believe this is why Jesus spoke of the coming of "he, the Spirit of Truth," of the coming of the "Comforter" and of the "Son of man."

Daniel's Prophecy

A newspaper article entitled "The Doomsday Syndrome" called attention to the beliefs of various denominations regarding the "end of time." Many seemed to agree that the signs of those "days" were abundant. Some set the year 2000 as "the time."

The article mentioned the belief of the Millerites (forerunners of the Seventh Day Adventists) that 1843 or 1844 was the "end of time." It is interesting to note that during the last century many biblical scholars used Daniel's prophecies of the "seventy weeks" (9:24) and the "2300 days" (8:14) to determine both the first and second coming of Christ. Their findings coincided with that of the Millerites. One in particular, which I found in a book published in 1881 titled *Thoughts Critical and Practical on the Books of Daniel and the Revelation,* by Uriah Smith, explains both appearances of Christ.

Starting with the decree of Artaxerxes in 457 B.C. authorizing the rebuilding of the Temple (Ezra, chapter 7) and using the biblical day as a year (Ezekiel 4:6 and Numbers 14:34), he found that the seventy weeks (7 x 70 equals 490 days) came to 33 A.D., the approximate time of Christ's crucifixion.

Using the same system for the 2300 days (2300 days from 457 B.C. equals 1843), he concluded that the "time of the end" began in 1844. The difference of one year is due to the fact that it takes 457 full years before Christ and 1843 full years after to make 2300, so that if the period commenced with the first day of 457 B.C., it would not terminate until the last day of 1843.

Those who opposed Smith's view said, "The 2300 years have not ended because the time has passed and the Lord has not come." His reaction was that although he couldn't understand why the Lord had not appeared, the 2300 days (years) had definitely gone by. "We therefore say again, with not a misgiving as to the truth of the assertion, not a fear of its successful contradiction, those days have ended."

Uriah Smith's comments are not without merit, because 1844 marked the beginning of a new world religion: the Bahá'í Faith, in Persia. It is world-wide in its scope, having members from nearly every national or ethnic background. Its founder, Bahá'u'lláh (Arabic for "the Glory of God"), claimed to be the "Spirit of Truth" promised by Jesus 2000 years ago.

Another interesting prophecy concerns the "forty and two months" and "a thousand two hundred and three score days" mentioned in the Book of Revelation (11:2-3). Both periods of time, using a day as a year, total 1260. 1260 in the Muslim calendar was the year 1844 In the Gregorian calendar.

Signs of the True Prophet

The Bible gives us warnings against false prophets and also reveals the signs of the true prophet who is to come in our time. By recognizing these signs mankind will be able to recognize him. According to scripture, a false prophet is one who speaks in the name of the Lord, but what he says does not come to pass (Deuteronomy 18:22). Scripture also tells us that the true prophet (the Christ Spirit in human form) will have a new name (Revelation 3:12). He will make all things new (Revelation 21:5), bringing the "new wine" which the old bottles cannot contain (Mark 2:22).

The Bible tells us we cannot know the hour in which he will come, but it does say (in the words of Jesus) that we must be awake and ready (Matthew 24:42). If we fail to recognize the signs of his coming, we could be in the same condition as were the Jews 2,000 years ago.

It is apparent that only a few shall recognize him at first, for history, including religious history, repeats itself. Thus the elect, for whom these days of tribulation shall be shortened (Matthew 24:22), will be few. These are the sheep who shall know his voice (John 10:4). Eventually all will become his sheep, "and there shall be one fold, and one shepherd" (John 10:16).

According to Jesus he will come as the "Son of man," this time from east of the Holy Land (Matthew 24:27, Ezekiel 43:2, 4). In Micah 7:12, we learn that he will come to the Holy Land "from Assyria, and from the fortified cities, and from the fortress even to the river, and from sea to sea, and from mountain to mountain."

One of the most significant of the signs of the "time of the end" is the return of the Jews to their homeland, which began as long ago as 1844 when the Turkish Government signed the historic Edict of Toleration permitting Jews to return to Palestine in freedom and security. Jesus referred to this sign of his return in Luke 21:24: "And they [the Jews] shall fall by the edge of the sword, and shall be led away captive into all nations: and Jerusalem shall be trodden down of the Gentiles, until the times of the Gentiles be fulfilled." Isaiah foresaw this great sign too: "And it shall come to pass in that day, that the Lord shall set his hand again the second time to recover the remnant of his people.... And he shall set up an ensign for the nations, and shall assemble the outcasts of Israel, and gather together the dispersed of Judah from the four corners of the earth" (11:11-12).

The New Name

I have written about the possibility of the return of Christ without his being recognized, as it happened two thousand years ago, when most of those to whom he preached, including the religious leaders, failed to know him. I have mentioned certain prophecies which have warned us to be awake and to watch.

Now I would like to show, from my understanding of the Bible, other reasons why Christ might come without being recognized. Some people believe that all will recognize him, which, in this day of international TV, could be possible. But, remember, seeing is not believing. He spoke in parables because "they seeing, see not; and hearing they hear not, neither do they understand" (Matthew 13:13). Seeing Christ, therefore, is not "receiving" him, that is, not accepting him.

He warned the people against false prophets, who would come saying, "I am Christ." Perhaps one of the reasons he warned us was because he knew he would return under a different name. In Revelation 3:12, he is recorded as saying, "And I will write upon him the name of my God, and the name of the city of my God, which is New Jerusalem, which cometh down out of heaven from my God: and I will write upon him my new name." In Revelation 2:17, he speaks of a white stone with a new name written in it, "which no man knoweth saving he that receiveth it." "Receiving it" means understanding it.

The Holy or Christ Spirit was hidden within the physical body of Jesus. Most failed to "receive" him because they thought he was an ordinary man like themselves. After all, "Can there any good thing come out of Nazareth?" (John 1:46). Is it possible then, that when he comes "in the clouds of heaven," he might not be recognized because the "cloud" of his human body, clad in a new name, hides the light of that spiritual Sun, the Holy Spirit, that is within? I believe it has already happened.

Christ Will Return From The East

While Jews and Christians focus their attention on the Holy Land in their religious thinking, they could be missing the one they are expecting. My study of the Bible indicates that the "return" of Christ is to be from east of the Holy Land. For example: "And, behold, the glory of the God of Israel came from the way of the east" (Ezekiel 43:2); "For as the lightning cometh out of the east, and shineth even unto the west: so shall also the coming of the Son of man be" (Matthew 24:27).

The implication of these prophecies is that Christ on his return might be of a people who are not Jews or Christians, for that part of Asia consists mostly of Muslims. The prophet Jeremiah (49:38) prophesied that God would set His "throne in Elam," present-day Iran, which is east of the Holy Land. And Micah (7:12) prophesied that "he shall come even to thee from Assyria, and from the fortified cities, and from the fortress even to the river, and from sea to sea, and from mountain to mountain." One of these mountains to be visited by the Promised One is Mt. Carmel in the Holy Land, for Isaiah (35:2) has foretold that "the excellency of Carmel and Sharon, they shall see the glory of the Lord, and the excellency of our God."

Across the bay from Mt. Carmel lies the fortress city of 'Akká (Achor in the Old Testament). The Prophet Hosea (2:15) predicted that it would have a glorious destiny: "And I will give her her vineyards from thence, and the valley of Achor for a door of hope." Isaiah (65:10) prophesied that "the valley of Achor shall be "a place for the herds to lie down in, for my people that have sought me." 'Akká, then, which is far to the west of Elam, or Iran, could be the final destination of the Promised One.

⌗⌗⌗⌗⌗⌗⌗⌗⌗⌗⌗⌗⌗⌗⌗⌗⌗⌗⌗⌗⌗

God's Kingdom

⌗⌗⌗⌗⌗⌗⌗⌗⌗⌗⌗⌗⌗⌗⌗⌗⌗⌗⌗⌗⌗

God's Plan

In meditating on the scriptures, seeking evidence that God has a plan for mankind on earth, my conclusion is that He does have such a plan and that He has spelled it out. The scriptures speak plainly on this subject. In the Book of Isaiah (2:4), telling of the coming of the Lord "in the last days," it is recorded, "And he (the Lord) shall judge among the nations, and shall rebuke many people: and they shall beat their swords into plowshares, and their spears into pruninghooks: nation shall not lift up sword against nation, neither shall they learn war any more."

This tells me that at the time of the end God's plan will come into fruition, and men will live in peace everywhere. Many people, clergymen included, believe we are now in "the last days." We seem far from the day when nations will learn war no more, but it is in times like these that God makes Himself evident in the affairs of men. This can be seen in the coming of Jesus 2,000 years ago, when God spoke to mankind in those "last days . . . by His Son" (Hebrews 1:2).

Turning to the New Testament, I found that Jesus, like Isaiah, spoke of God's plan. He told of the coming together of all people into one fold (John 10:16), and he prayed for the advent of God's kingdom on earth (Matthew 6:10). Who, believing Jesus, can doubt that his prayer will be answered?

Jesus knew that mankind would suffer greatly and that this suffering would be the purging of men, causing them to return to God once more. In Matthew, chapter 24, he spells out the calamities to come at the "end of the world." The "end of the world" is the same as the "last days." It means (even as it did in Hebrews 1:2) the end of one religious cycle and the beginning of a new one. Thus God's plan entails a cyclical renewal of religion that is to culminate in the unity of all mankind in one universal religion. Nothing less than this can bring about the kingdom of God on earth.

The Promise of Peace

Every once in a while I hear someone saying, "There will always be wars. That's God's way of keeping the world from becoming overpopulated." I have two reasons for not accepting this statement. First, we had wars when the world wasn't over-populated. Second, the purpose of man is to bring peace on earth, to fulfill the prophecy of Jesus that we would become as one fold. Man is the instrument for this heavenly work.

God has made covenants throughout the ages with man as he advanced toward his destiny. "Have we not all one Father? Hath not one God created us? Why do we deal treacherously every man against his brother, by profaning the covenant of our fathers?" (Malachi 2:10).

The Psalms tell us: "Behold how good and pleasant it is for brethren to dwell together in unity!" (133:1). Is it possible that God uses war to diminish His creation on earth? Not if one really believes the Bible. It says that we will beat our military instruments into plowshares and into pruning hooks, and that nations will no longer make war with each other. God is to teach us of His ways, and we will walk in His path (Isaiah 2:3-4).

Jesus spoke of wars and rumors of wars, but he also said that "for the elect's sake those days shall be shortened (Matthew

24:22). I take it to mean that those who learn God's ways and obey His laws will keep the world from being destroyed. If this were not so, how would it be possible for mankind to become the one fold promised by Jesus (John 10:16)?

God Is In Command

People ask me how I can feel so positive in this mixed-up negative world of ours, and I reply that I know God is still in command on earth. I look upon this as the day of reckoning, the day in which, as the Dead Sea scrolls have revealed, the final battle between "the children of light" and "the children of darkness" is being fought. According to the scrolls, it is the battle in which God intervenes to bring victory to the children of light.

The children of darkness are those who resist change. Referring to this battle, Dr. Martin Luther King Jr. said, "The struggle is due to those who cling tenaciously to a world that no longer exists." "The dying old world order," as he called it, is opposed to the new world order, the birth of which he claimed was coming into being. The children of darkness cling to their prejudices, be they racial, religious, or patriotic, forgetting that mankind was made "of one blood" (Acts 17:26).

Also speaking of the children of darkness, Dr. Firuz Kazem-zadeh, Associate Professor of History at Yale University, wrote, "Man's torment is a result of his stubborn unwillingness to recognize his spiritual nature and the nature of the spiritual laws which govern him."

Jesus foretold of the time of the final victory of the children of light with his promise of the day of the one fold. God, patient as He has been with His disobedient creation, will have the final say on the victory of good over evil. An example of the triumph of good over evil can be seen in a statement by Dr. King, in which he said, "Evil may so shape events that Caesar may occupy a palace and Christ a cross, but one day that Christ will rise up and split history into B.C. and A.D., so that even the life of Caesar must be dated by his (Christ's) name."

That the good suffer because of the evil is nothing new. The life and death of Jesus proves it. My optimism in this "mixed-up" world stems from my understanding that this is God's method of purifying mankind. He is in command of the world.

The One Fold

I believe I know how Christ's prophecy of the one fold will be fulfilled. It will be when all mankind recognizes the Spirit of Truth, who is to guide us into all truth. He will gather all of the sheep from all the different "folds" (religions) and bring them together into one fold.

The kingdom of God cannot be realized on earth until the world awakens to the truth that all religions are really different dispensations of the one religion of God. Before we can become so unified, we must search out the similarities in each other's beliefs instead of condemning one another because of insignificant outward differences, usually the rituals and dogmas. After all, everyone who worships God worships the one God. "Hear, O Israel: the Lord our God is one Lord" (Deuteronomy 6:4).

The Kingdom of God

If we believe the beloved Jesus, we must also believe that the day will come when the kingdom of God shall reign on earth. Jesus prayed for it, and his prayers will be answered.

What will that kingdom be like? Well, in this day and age it is impossible to get the full impact of such a glorious condition. For sure, the peoples of the earth will worship God and love their fellowmen. But, material minds like ours cannot absorb the spiritual glory of such a day. The Bible explains this: "Eye hath not seen, nor ear heard, neither have entered into the heart of man, the things which God hath prepared for them that love him" (I Corinthians 2:9).

Perhaps people will attain to such spirituality as to make them like prophets, not unlike the Hebrew prophets of ages ago.

Moses may have visualized such a station for mankind, and at least, hoped for it. He said, "Would God that all the Lord's people were prophets, and that the Lord would put his spirit upon them" (Numbers 11:29).

It seems that God did act on that hope. In Joel, 2:28-29, God is quoted as saying, "And it shall come to pass afterward, that I will pour out my spirit upon all flesh; and your sons and your daughters shall prophesy, your old men shall dream dreams, your young men shall see visions; And also upon the servants and upon the handmaidens in those days will I pour out my spirit." "Those days" will be the days of God's kingdom on earth.

Isaiah gives further evidence of that glorious day to come, saying, "Thy people also shall be all righteous: they shall inherit the land for ever, the branch of my planting, the work of my hands, that I (God) may be glorified" (60:21).

We are born too soon for that glorious day to come, but we can do our part in bringing it closer by loving God and our fellowmen. This, I believe, is our purpose for living. It is only by making the world a little better than it was when we were born that we can justify our lives on earth.

The Old Order Is Passing Away

The readers of this column know that I often write of my belief that we are living in the "time of the end" when we are to be led into all truth (John 16:13). Another person who believed likewise was Dr. Martin Luther King Jr. In a speech in Montgomery, Alabama, on December 3, 1956, he said, "The old order is passing away and the new order is coming into being. We are witnessing in our day the birth of a new age, with a structure of freedom and justice."

According to the Essenes, who wrote what became known as the Dead Sea scrolls, there were to be seven battles between the forces of good and the forces of evil. Each was to win three battles, and then in the seventh battle, the forces of good were to win. As I see it, we are in that last battle.

Dr. King knew that this new age would not come without a

struggle. He said, "It is both historically and biologically true that there can be no birth and growth without birth pains and growing pains. Whenever there is the emergence of the new, we confront the recalcitrance of the old. So the tensions which we witness in the world today are indicative of the fact that a new order is being born and an old world order is passing away."

Dr. King foresaw the day of the one fold. In that same speech in Montgomery, he said that our world is now geographically one, and that our challenge is to make it spiritually one. When it becomes spiritually one, we shall be as one fold. His confidence in this belief was due to his strong belief in God. He was convinced that the universe is under the control of a Loving Purpose, and that in the struggle for righteousness man has cosmic companionship. "Behind the harsh appearances of the world there is a benign power." He realized that the divine Power (God) was working in history to bring about this new age.

This Unparalleled Age

If you don't realize that you are living in the most unusual time in history, you don't understand this age. It is an age of unparalleled progress. This age is moving so fast, few people can keep up with it. For example, we have developed unprecedented methods of communication, and yet wars and our inability to get along with each other throughout the world prove that we are not communicating.

We are living in a day in which we must raise our sights up to universal unity in order to keep from destroying our world. Instead, we continue to cling to the lesser unities of nation, race, and social castes, which do not suffice for this universal age. There is a crying need for universal unity.

If one looks upon universal unity as being an unattainable goal, then one must become aware of two facts: such a unity has been promised by the founders of all the past revelations from God, and we have been given the means to bring it about, namely modern communication and transportation, which have shrunk our vast world into a neighborhood. Modern armaments make it imperative for us to bring that unity into being.

I believe that when God gives us the instruments for our development, He means for us to use them. Therefore, we no longer have any excuse for putting off the building of the kingdom of God on earth. It is a job in which the majority of people will have to take part. Those who refuse to labor in this vineyard will suffer for their laxity.

It is not surprising that many fail to read the signs of this unparalleled age. Jesus found the people in the same condition 2,000 years ago. He rebuked them, saying, "O ye hypocrites, ye can discern the face of the sky; but can ye not discern the signs of the times?" (Matthew 16:3).

The Stage of Maturity

All created things have their degree or stage of maturity. For instance, the period of maturity in the life of a tree is the time of its fruit-bearing. Man reaches his maturity when his intelligence is at its peak.

From the beginning of a person's life until its end, he or she passes through certain periods or stages. The condition and requirements of childhood are different from the conditions and requirements of youth. As he or she grows into adulthood, the limitations of the earlier life must be given up for mature activities, as each person finds new powers and perceptions, and teaching and training that go along with the progression of maturity occupies the mind. The former period of youth and its conditions will no longer satisfy a person of matured view and vision.

The apostle Paul spoke of the spiritual maturing of men. Referring to the believers as "babes in Christ," he said, "I have fed you with milk, and not with meat: for hitherto ye were not able to bear it, neither yet now are ye able" (I Corinthians 3:2). He was referring to their being envious, with strife and divisions among them. In Hebrews 5:13, Paul points out their spiritual immaturity once more: "For every one that useth milk is unskillful in the word of righteousness: for he is a babe."

Speaking of spiritual maturity, he said, "But strong meat belongeth to them that are of full age, even those who by reason of use have their senses exercised to discern both good and evil" (Hebrews 5:14).

The spiritual maturity of mankind must be nurtured by a continuous revelation of religion, for as man grows, he can grasp a greater portion of truth. Religious truth is relative, each consecutive age bringing more of it to grasp. Things we could not bear 2,000 years ago (John 16:12) are self-evident today. That which was applicable to human needs during the early history of the human race neither meets nor satisfies the demands of this day, and it is for this reason that the various religions are awaiting another Teacher from God.

In this day, when the world seems to be falling apart spiritually men must, I believe, become mature in order to save it from impending destruction. Maturity is to life what a steering wheel is to an automobile; it keeps men on the straight and narrow, avoiding the pitfalls of selfishness and greed. To date, few men have reached the maturity needed to fully advance civilization to the degree where all could live in peace and tranquility, even though the great Teachers of each age (the most mature of men) have revealed the blueprints of a perfect society from time immemorial.

The tragedy of life up to now has been the failure of men in general to understand these Teachers. In fact, because of mankind's immaturity, the Teachers have been vilified and persecuted. An immature person dislikes change because new teachings challenge his way of life and threaten his ego.

Today we are living in an age that demands maturity from men. The crux of our problems is that time is running out on us, a situation that couldn't arise in past ages. It is but a few years since scientists discovered nuclear power, which, in the hands of immature people, can literally destroy our world. As a Bible student, I believe that Armaggedon is the battle between the mature and the immature.

We are living in the age to which Jesus referred when he said we would be guided into the "all truth" (maturity), which men could not bear 2,000 years ago. Jesus knew that his sufferings at the hands of those who crucified him was not due to evil, but to immaturity. This explains his words on the cross: "Father, forgive them; for they know not what they do" (Luke 23:34).

The Unity of Mankind

The purpose of God's Teachers throughout the ages has been to bring His creation, the human race, together in unity. This means that eventually all the peoples of the world will serve God "with one consent" (Zephaniah 3:9).

In order to work toward world unity, we must understand what unity means. My dictionary says that unity means "the state of being one; singleness; concord; harmony . . ." This theme of unity is proclaimed in every religion. In the Old Testament: "Have we not all one Father? Hath not one God created us?" (Malachi 2:10). In the New Testament we have the promise of Jesus that mankind will become one fold under one shepherd (John 10:16). In the Qur'án Muhammad, promises that "all mankind shall be gathered together" in "the latter day" (Súra 11:105).

The unity of the world of nature, created by God, is an example of how mankind should exist spiritually. The one sun, the physical light of the world, shines on everyone: good and evil. Without that one sun, nothing would be able to exist on earth. God is the one Spiritual Sun, without whose bounty and mercy we would not have been created. He wishes to be worshipped alone, and the day is coming when He will be, thanks to the educating influence of His prophets, for "in that day there shall be one Lord, and his name one" (Zechariah 14:9).

Recognizing Our Oneness

One of my favorite pastimes is meditating on Bible prophecy for the purpose of discovering how it might be fulfilled. Many people believe that prophecy will be fulfilled when Christ comes, and that he will automatically transform the world.

I do agree with the point that when the Christ comes his appearance will trigger the transformation of the world, but not automatically, because mass acceptance of God's Teachers comes only many years after their ascension. Only a few accept the prophets when they are on earth, and for many years these Teachers are considered to be false prophets and their followers heretics. How is it then that Christ's promises for the coming of the kingdom on earth will be fulfilled?

This fulfillment will occur as each man recognizes and adheres to the admonitions of God's Teacher for this new Day. Consider the prophecy of the "one fold." The "one fold" will mark the complete unification of mankind on earth; then "shall there be one Lord and his name one" (Zechariah 14:9). "For then will I turn to the people a pure language, that they may all call upon the name of the Lord, to serve him with one consent" (Zephaniah 3:9).

The prophecy of the "one fold" will be fulfilled through the unification of mankind. This will happen when humanity recognizes that all of God's Teachers are endowed with the Holy Spirit. The followers of each religion will cast off their religious prejudice in the same manner that, by recognizing the oneness of all humanity, people will rid themselves of racial prejudice. Although it may take a few centuries to achieve this goal, each succeeding generation will accelerate the trend toward it.

Unity of Nations

United Nations Day is celebrated on October 24. Although there is controversy in the world, indeed, in our own country, as to the advisability of a unity of nations in one international agency, it is apparent that such an organization is necessary. The need is as urgent today as it was 200 years ago for the confederation of states to become the United States of America. Had the states refused to federate, our country would have become a maze of small countries like those in Europe, with the exception, possibly, of a common tongue, but with conflicting laws. Imagine needing a passport to travel from state to state!

Each age brings a new, higher form of unity as the world evolves and progresses. At the time of Abraham, the family was the highest unit of social life. Moses brought tribal unity, which was followed in the days of Jesus by city-state unity. Muhammad's day marked the beginning of national unity, and in this day, who can deny the need for a still higher unity—universal unity—the highest form possible on this planet.

Albert Einstein, whose genius ushered in the nuclear age, pointed out the weakness of national unity in a universal age, saying, "Nationalism is an infantile disease. It is the measles of mankind." Well, we've grown up! The lower forms of unity in this age are like milk, and universal unity is like the strong meat which, according to St. Paul, is reserved for those who are mature enough to discern good from evil (Hebrews 5:14).

I visualize the true United Nations of the future as a spiritually oriented agency built on a plan of federation similar to that which brought all of the states of our country together. I believe we will see this organization in full working order as soon as the nations of the world learn to put aside their own selfish short-term interests for the imperative needs of a rapidly integrating planet.

The End of Nationalism

Nationalism will soon be as outmoded as the covered wagon. For unless the world is able to unite in an international form of government, disaster will result. Universal cooperation is needed for survival. It is my belief that an international government will develop in the same manner as did the federation of the original United States. The federation did not come easy. There was much argument and disagreement before the unity came, but it was destined to be.

The nations of the world will unite, if for no other reason than the course of present events: the growing incidence of crime, the disruption of the environment on a global scale, world famine, international terrorism, etc. These things will force mankind together to solve its own problems, and to heed the truths taught by God's messengers, especially the golden rule. As Muhammad stated it in the Qur'án: "No one of you is a believer until he desires for his brother that which he desires for himself."

Isolation and separation are becoming increasingly impossible. Those who, perhaps for understandable reasons, advocate separation will find that it cannot continue in this shrinking world. In the near future we will be forced to recognize that "united we stand, divided we fall" on a universal scale. Already the world is interdependent in economic and political spheres.

Unity in Diversity

Man is diverse and man is one: diverse in physical attributes and one in creation. We all recognize the physical differences, but are only slowly accepting the oneness of mankind. This knowledge grows as we awaken spiritually and begin to understand that golden image of God instilled (and often stilled) within our souls. Unless we take a mature attitude toward the diversities of humanity, we cannot understand our essential oneness and we will not be able to deal successfully with the urgent problems of the world.

Dr. N. J. Berrill, in his book *You and the Universe,* ably states the question: "We see a different face in every human being, yet behind them all we see the same person whether their skin be yellow, brown or white, or whether they be men or women. The diversity is there without a doubt but so is the essential oneness. Nobody seriously questions the family of man or the fundamental brotherhood. In fact, the present human problem, though by no means the only one, is how to accept and adjust to the all-pervading diversity in such a way that the underlying unity predominates."

The answer to this problem is as old as the problem itself. Every prophet of God has spoken of it. God said, "Love thy neighbor as thyself" (Leviticus 19:18). In Malachi 2:10, it is recorded, "Have we not all one father? Hath not one God created us?" Jesus said, "Love your enemies, bless them that curse you" (Matthew 5:44). Muhammad said, "Mankind was but one people; and God sent prophets to announce glad-tidings and to warn; and He sent down with them the Book of Truth, that it might decide the disputes of men" (Qur'án 2:209). Thus we have always been admonished to accept unity despite our diversities. The important point is this: Give loving service, not lip service.

A Wider Love

The world is overrun with hate, greed, and violence, and it seems doomed because of the modern armaments held by nations of diverse ideologies. Families are breaking up; we are not safe in our own homes, and we see affluent persons dabbling in drugs and fraud.

Occasionally I hear the song "What the World Needs Now is Love, Sweet Love" on the radio. There are many forms of love—love for one's family, love for one's religion, love for one's ethnic group—but these are limited loves which can have no lasting results. In this universal age it is universal love that is needed in order to eliminate the hate, the greed, and the violence presently in vogue.

Martin Luther King Jr. explained vividly the kind of love we need. He said, "The highest level of love is that of agape. Agape means nothing sentimental or basically affectionate. It means understanding, redeeming goodwill which asks nothing in return. It is the love of God working in the lives of men.

"When we rise to love on the agape level, we love men, not because we like them, not because their attitudes and ways appeal to us, but because God loves them. Here we rise to the position of loving the person who does the evil deed, while hating the deed that the person does. With this type of love—understanding goodwill—we will be able to stand amid the glow of the new age with dignity and discipline."

Dr. King's words helped me to understand what Jesus taught: "Love your enemies, bless them that curse you" (Matthew 5:44). This is a difficult thing to do, but it is an edict from God. If we become dutiful children, obeying our Heavenly

Father's admonitions, we will begin to understand the wisdom of agape love.

Jesus prayed, "Thy kingdom come. Thy will be done in earth, as it is in heaven" (Matthew 6:10). God's will on earth must come through mankind's obedience to Him. We are the instruments who are to bring God's plan for this earth into fruition. It cannot be done without our acceptance of agape love.

How Peace Will Come

Mankind should be concentrating on ways to bring peace to the world. We seem to be as far away as ever from peace, but we mustn't cease striving for it. Before we can have peace we must have unity. In II Corinthians 13:11, it is recorded: "Be of one mind, live in peace; and the God of love and peace shall be with you." It is only when we are of one mind—in unity—that peace can be achieved. The Bible rejects that "old wives' tale" that war is God's way of keeping the world from becoming overpopulated. War is confusion, and "God is not the author of confusion, but of peace" (I Corinthians 14:33).

One of our difficulties in achieving peace is that we are waiting for others to provide it for us. Peace, like every other good thing, begins at home through training. Working toward peace is a slow process, but we must make a beginning if we are to accomplish it. In the words of President John F. Kennedy, "Peace is a daily, a weekly, a monthly process, gradually changing opinions, slowly eroding old barriers, quietly building new structures."

The enemies of peace are greed and the desire for power. Some individuals believe that they should dominate the world. History proves that such power-drunk persons and their regimes eventually collapse and disintegrate. We have two recent examples of this process—in Haiti and the Philippines. All the power held by Duvalier and Marcos left them. God has his timetable and no human being can turn it back. Greed and power, as well as untruth, are the enemies of peace, but they cannot stand the test of time.

Truth is like a rubber ball being held under water. As soon as it is released, it will pop up forcefully. One cannot hold it down forever. Dictators crush truth, but not forever. In the words of William Cullen Bryant, American poet and historian of the eighteenth century, "Truth crushed to earth shall rise again."

Is it possible to achieve universal peace? Many people say, "No way! There have always been wars and there will always be wars." On the other hand, those who believe in Bible scripture would say, "Yes, peace is sure to come." Here are some reasons. Has not Isaiah promised, "Nation shall not lift up sword against nation, neither shall they learn war any more" (2:4). Isaiah also promised the coming of the Prince of Peace (9:6). If there is to be no peace, what would be the need for the Prince of Peace? If there is a Prince, then there must be a kingdom, and his kingdom is the promised kingdom of God on earth. Jesus said that on that day "there shall be one fold, and one shepherd" (John 10:16).

One might ask, "When will peace come?" Under present world conditions many would say, "Not today. Maybe in a thousand years or so." I dispute this line of thought. Although building peace is a gradual process, the pillars of its mighty structure are already being established. The thought of East and West is realigning toward common goals. International organizations and international undertakings are proliferating in the economic, environmental, and humanitarian spheres of life. Victor Hugo (1820-85) wrote of the twentieth century: "For all, there will be but one country—that country the whole world: for all there will be one hope—that hope the whole heaven."

H. A. Overstreet, noted psychologist, wrote that the central problem of our day is "that of moving out of provincialism into one world. . . . There can be no doubt that the key problem of our period is that of expressing through adequate political and legal institutions the oneness of the human race." However, I don't expect that peace will endure through political or legal institutions alone. Enduring unity in the material realm is dependent upon a universal inner unity of spirit and thought. As Lecomte Du Noüy perceived in his book *Human Destiny:* "The happiness of people depends in part on the unity of religious thought. The world will believe in peace when the churches demonstrate that it can exist."

The Power of Prayer for Peace

As individuals most of us feel incapable of changing the materialistic trend of the world, which is fraught with dishonesty and immorality. I used to feel that way, too; but now I believe there is a secret weapon available to each one of us. When used with spirit and with love for God, we can change the world if sufficient numbers arm themselves with this weapon.

I am speaking of prayer. The Old and New Testaments bear witness to the importance of prayer. Jesus told us how to pray when he revealed the Lord's Prayer (Matthew 6:9-13). He also promised: "And all things, whatsoever ye shall ask in prayer, believing, ye shall receive" (Matthew 21:22). If we yearn for peace and for the promised kingdom of God, let us use sincere prayer in growing numbers to help peace become a reality. Temper prayer with the love of God and the love of one's fellowmen. As Coleridge wrote, "He prayeth best who loveth best." Buddha said that the greatest prayer is patience. Yes, we must be patient while awaiting answers to our prayers, but, at the same time, we mustn't be idle while waiting. Faith without works is dead.

It has been said that we must pray as if all the work in the world won't help, and work as if all the prayer in the world won't help. Jeremy Taylor wrote, "Whatsoever we beg of God, let us also work for it." As I see it, the real work is to develop ourselves spiritually so that we will be deserving of a peaceful world. Thus, the mystery of praying is that we answer our prayers by becoming what we are praying for.

As the world continues to darken it becomes evident that the combined wisdom of mankind, unaided by God, is not sufficient for the work of bringing peace to earth. Abraham Lincoln knew this, saying, "I have been driven many times to my knees by the overwhelming conviction that I had no where else to go. My own wisdom, and that of all about me, seemed insufficient for the day."

The Law of Change

In this world nothing is permanent but change. We human beings are continually changing, from our development in the womb until we die. We cannot stop change and we shouldn't try. We are placed on earth, obliged to change physically, and given free will to change spiritually in order to make this a better world and to prepare ourselves for the world beyond. If we refuse to make such changes, we may be committing "spiritual suicide."

John F. Kennedy, in an address made in 1963, said, "Change is the law of life. And those who look only to the past or the present are certain to miss the future." This can be seen in those who wave Confederate flags and hold to racial prejudice. Such people are still living in the nineteenth century. The world is passing them by, but they don't seem to know it. We need a "time machine" to bring them up to date.

This concept of change is not new. Heraclitis (ca. 500 B.C.) described change in this way: "You cannot step twice in the same river, for other waters are continually flowing in." Martin Luther King hit the nail on the head when he said, "The world is changing and anyone who thinks he can live alone is sleeping through a revolution." He was referring to the "dying of the old world order and the birth of a new world order of justice and freedom." He pointed out that sacrifices were needed to make the transition from the old to the new, and he made the supreme sacrifice as an example.

Our local, national, and international problems indicate that we are in the transitional period. Over 150 years ago John C. Calhoun, Vice-President of the United States in 1825-1832, wrote, "The interval between the decay of the old and the formation and the establishment of the new, constitutes a period of transition, which must always necessarily be one of uncertainty, confusion, error and wild and fierce fanaticism." This is an accurate picture of our changing world today.

The *Miami Times* is cognizant of our changing world. Its masthead reads: "Tempora Mutantur Et Nos Mutamur in Ilis," which, translated, means "The times are changed and we are changed with it."

Spiritual Light Precedes Physical Light

This column is being written just a few days after the one hundreth anniversary of the invention of the incandescent light bulb. I want to comment on this "en-light-ening" invention and its relationship to spiritual light.

According to my religious belief spiritual light must come before physical light. Every good thing that comes to this world first existed in the spiritual world—the world of God. For example: In the first chapter of Genesis, it is related that the light of day appeared on the first day (1:3-5) but that the sun did not appear until the third day (1:14). It isn't possible to have the light of day in the physical world without the sun. My contention is that the light of the first two days of creation was spiritual light, preparing the world for the appearance of the light of the sun. The spiritual light was the Word of God, which was "in the beginning" (John 1:1).

Long before Edison invented the electric light bulb, it existed as an idea in the spiritual world, waiting for someone to bring it into the physical realm.

Another example of "inner light" preceding "outer light" can be seen in the workings of a camera. We know that as soon as a picture is taken, it is already present in the camera. However, it is only when the film is removed and developed that the picture becomes visible. This invention is a symbol of the power given by God to man to bring the heavenly things to light.

When Jesus prayed for the kingdom of God to come to earth, he was "exposing" the film of a spiritual camera. In order to behold this "heavenly picture," man must develop it. We have failed so far because we are still in a "negative" stage of spiritual development. However, we are living in the age when this "picture"—the kingdom of God on earth—can be developed. The condition of the world indicates that we are now in the "dark room" of development, but as we know, it is always darkest just before the dawn.

The Communication Gap

In this age of rapid-fire communications, the biggest problem we have is the communication gap. Lack of communication is a major cause of disputes between husband and wife; it is a wall of silence between parents and their children (the generation gap); it is distrust and suspicion that prevent true negotiations between nations, and it is a veil of prejudice which keeps mankind divided by class, creed, and color.

Although these communication gaps contribute to our worldly ills, in the final analysis they are not so much causes as they are effects of a more serious gap: the communication gap between man and his Maker. Because of this gap, man has weakened his initiative to communicate with his fellowmen, be it his spouse, his off-spring, those of other nations or of other colors or creeds. If we do not communicate with our Maker, how then are we to communicate with His creation? We are all created (latently) in His image, and this should enable us to communicate with each other.

Where have we failed? Why is it that we have been able to fashion so many amazing technological products for our material benefit, not the least of which are such communication devices as the telephone, TV, and Telestar, yet fail to communicate on a person-to-person basis?

I believe it is because of the lack of communication between man's mind and his heart. He uses the mind (the seat of material intelligence) without consulting the heart (the seat of humanitarian intelligence). What man must do now is eliminate the communication gap between mind and heart. Then will the heart guide the material intelligence so it will benefit all mankind, fostering love and unity instead of hate and separation, for "As in water face answereth to face, so the heart of man to man" (Proverb 27:19).

The Puzzle of Life

As I look at life, I think back to the days when I enjoyed working jigsaw puzzles. I believe that the interest I took in fitting the pieces together to get the picture provided me with sufficient curiosity to attempt to get the picture of life once I took interest in my fellowmen and in world events.

Now as I reflect on life I see a striking similarity between life and a jigsaw puzzle. Our Creator has made us into one universal puzzle, with each of us a piece that belongs in the picture. Like pieces of a puzzle, we come in all sizes, shapes, and colors. In my estimation, the best jigsaw puzzles are the most colorful ones. Racists attempt to make the picture of humanity entirely one color. Such attempts will end in failure because they are contrary to God's plan for humanity. There is no joy in doing a colorless picture. It is far more difficult to do, and if one has the patience to complete such a puzzle, the results will not be rewarding.

The jigsaw puzzle of life, when all the pieces are in their proper places, will be the most beautiful picture imaginable, since the Greatest Artist, God, designed it. Woe unto them who try to eliminate any piece from its proper place! Much blood has been shed, and will continue to be shed, until we all fit together into that colorful picture. Each piece of the universal puzzle, be it from the most remote Indian tribe of Bolivia to the Pigmies of Africa, or of an Eskimo village in the Arctic, is just as important, and adds as much color to the picture as does a piece representing our President or any other well-known person. Only when all learn this eternal truth will our puzzle be solved. Then we shall see the glorious picture of life as God created it.

The true artist takes great pains in perfecting the tiniest detail in his pictures. How much more does the Creator take care in His portrait of life! Hate scatters the pieces, but love attracts and fits them together in the plan of God. We must love our fellowmen. Then we will truly "get the picture."

America's Destiny

There are many forms of integration. Eventually, all shall lead to universal peace, the destiny of this planet. America progressed when its earliest settlers, fleeing from religious and political oppression in Europe, sought peace and freedom in the New World. Coming from various countries and cultures, they integrated easily with each other. Later, as separate political units or states, they were able to unite into one federal unit. Thus, we find that America has already set the pattern for an integrated world, the prerequisite of universal peace. Had her states not integrated she might yet be an English colony.

Today, in order to fulfill America's destiny as a leader amongst the nations in the pathway of universal peace, it must first purify itself of a great internal evil. This evil is racism and the increasing social separation of America's colored and white citizens. The rest of the world is watching us as we struggle to overcome this stumbling block, this irritating problem, without strife and violence.

Despite its ominous implications, the racial situation might be likened to the irritation that develops within an oyster, ending up as a precious pearl. When America matures sufficiently to overcome its racial prejudices, it will bring into being the priceless pearl of universal peace. Therefore, the destiny of America is interwoven with the destiny of its Black citizens. Together they shall rise or fall. When the racial problem is solved through the universal recognition of our common humanity, they will bring into fruition America's great destiny. In this world of predominately non-white people they will become our goodwill ambassadors, awakening the non-white nations to follow America into that golden era of universal peace that must come.

Utopia

The word "utopia" comes from the Greek, meaning "no-place." However, ironically, the term is used to describe a place where perfection in laws, government, and social conditions exists. Its denotative meaning is that such perfection can be found no where.

I believe, however, that the whole world will become a "utopia" in its symbolic sense, meaning, a place where such perfection will be found. Jesus said that humanity would become as one fold under one shepherd (John 10:16). But the components of that perfect world will only come into being when certain conditions are met. For instance, mankind must first recognize its oneness, for we are all children of the one Creator. Mankind must also become unified in one universal faith, brought by the "Spirit of Truth," whom Jesus said would guide us into all truth (John 16:13). Prejudice, be it racial, religious, or national, must vanish from the face of the earth. Education must be universal, children throughout the world being taught without racial or national bias. In our own country the history of the Civil War must no longer differ in the South from that in the North.

Science and religion must work hand in hand, the achievements of science being directed entirely to peaceful uses and the spiritual insights of religion being guided by reason. Equality of men and women must be achieved to the satisfaction of both, since each holds an equally important position in God's scheme of things. Already there is a world-wide effort to bring this about. A universal auxiliary language must be established, enabling world leaders to settle their differences with words instead of wars. About 300 efforts have been made so far toward creating such a language. Our economic problems must have a spiritual solution for, as we begin to live in harmony under God's laws, greed and the desire for power will become universally recognized as immature expressions of the human reality.

In order to safeguard these principles, a universal tribunal with the equal representation of all countries must be founded. Then, instead of "no-place," perfection in laws, government, and social conditions will exist "every-place." I'm sure the Greeks have a word for that!

"The World Dictator"?

A well-known evangelist said that because more and more countries are developing central governments; since the United Nations is becoming a world agency for government; and that with the development of communication satellites, one man can now speak to about eighty percent of the world at one time, we may expect the world dictatorship foretold in the Bible. To quote him: "What I am saying is that we are moving toward one-world government, one-world church, one-world labor union, and world-wide industries. All these are setting the stage for the world dictator prophesied in the Bible."

I presume he was referring to Revelation 13:7, which speaks of the beast whose power was to last forty-two months. "And it was given unto him to make war with the saints, and to overcome them: and power was given him over all kindreds, and tongues, and nations."

According to the Bible (Ezekiel 4:6 and Numbers 14:34) each "day" is a year in prophecy, so forty-two months would be 1260 years (42 x 30). Some Bible scholars have also interpreted the "time, times and a half" as being identical to the period of the dispensation of Muhammad. The year 1260 A.H. of the Muslim calendar equals the year 1844 of the Christian calendar. In that year the former cycle of God's religion ended and the new one began, the one promised in all the sacred scriptures as the Day of God Himself.

"The beast that ascendeth out of the bottomless pit" (Revelation 11:7) to make war against God's two witnesses, 'Ali and Muhammad, was the infamous Umayyad Dynasty that took hold of the reins of Islam, made war against the descendents of Muhammad, and subverted its divine foundation. The "woman clothed with the sun, and the moon under her feet" (Revelation 12:1) represents the Law of God brought by Muhammad. The emblem of Persia is the sun and that of the Ottoman empire the crescent moon: both kingdoms were under the sway of Islamic law, which was symbolically forced "into the wilderness" for 1260 years, until the coming of a new Teacher from God would revive it.

This interpretation of the revelation of St. John makes more sense as it takes into account the history and existence of Islam, a divinely inspired world faith that came to pass after the time of Christ. For one man to take control of the whole world and maintain his rule for 1,260 years in this age of complex political interdependency is a virtual impossibility.

The Purpose of Life

Man's Purpose in Life

Does life have a purpose? In my younger days this question disturbed me, and it was only when I turned to the Bible that I found suitable answers. In the scriptures man is likened to a fruit-bearing tree. In meditating on this thought, I realized that a tree that does not bear fruit is useless, "fit for the fire." Therefore, if a man does not "bear fruit" (fulfill his reason for being created), he too is a failure. In Matthew 21:19, Jesus, finding a fig tree without fruit on it, said, "Let no fruit grow on thee henceforth forever," and the tree withered.

Wondering what the fruits of men are, I searched through the Bible and found some answers. In Proverb 11:30, I read, "The fruit of the righteous is a tree of life." In Job 32:8, Elihu says, "There is a spirit in man." Ecclesiastes 12:7 tells us that "the spirit shall return unto God who gave it." I began to visualize that the God-given spirit was a seed from which the fruits of men are grown. A confirmation came from Galatians 5:22, where I read: "But the fruit of the Spirit is love, joy, peace, longsuffering, gentleness, goodness, faith." I recognized these as being attributes of God, who is a Spirit (John 4:24).

In the parable of the sower (Matthew 13:3-8) Jesus reveals

151

that only when a seed falls on good soil does it bring forth fruit. Therefore, man has to cleanse his heart of the rocky soil of self and hate so that it will enable the spirit (seed) to flourish. Thus, that spirit in man, when nurtured, bears the fruit of the tree of life, and helps man to attain everlasting life in the presence of God, who gave man life through that spirit.

Reflecting The Spiritual Sun

I believe we would have a clearer vision of what religion truly is if we looked at the important factors that enable us, as physical beings, to live on earth. For instance, we know that it is through the constant shining of the sun that life of all kinds, including human life, can exist on earth.

The Bible tells us that we are spiritual beings as well as physical beings. God is the Spiritual Sun who gives us spiritual sustenance. Now, the physical sun does not come down to earth, but instead sends its lifegiving rays to do the job. Nor does God, the Spiritual Sun, come down to earth. Instead, He sends His "rays"—the Holy Spirit—in human form, a Moses, Jesus, or Muhammad, to provide us with the means for spiritual birth (being "born again") in preparation for the glorious mansions in the world beyond.

Not all humans attain this spiritual station, but all have the free will to strive for it. We are like mirrors, and in order to reflect perfectly the spiritual "rays" from God, each must cleanse his or her "mirror" of the dust of prejudice, greed, and attachment to worldly things. Such "dust" will ultimately keep us from accepting and reflecting the Holy Spirit.

It is only when we consciously strive to receive those life-giving "rays" that they will be reflected in our lives. It may be that by the grace of God we become conscious of Him, but it is only through our own volition and works that we are enabled to reflect His attributes, such as truthfulness, faithfulness, and sanctity. As Christ admonished his followers, "Let your light so shine before men that they may see your good works, and glorify your Father which is in heaven" (Matthew 5:16).

Transform Yourself First

We see the world around us collapsing, dying of the cancers of greed, hate, war, and crime, and we wonder what can each of us do to turn things around and make this a better world. In meditating on this dilemma, I came up with the realization that the only thing I can change in this world is myself. However, there is a little magic in self-improvement, because by doing so, I actually change those around me. By making myself more pleasant, more lovable, and more considerate of others, they change right along with me. The magic happens because I become a different person in their eyes, and therefore they are drawn toward me, where before they were withdrawn. Others react toward me according to the way I act toward them.

It isn't easy to change ourselves, weak human beings that we are. To make a radical change in one's self one must turn to God, the All-Powerful, who has the ability. Only He can inspire us to change. He sent Moses and Jesus, among others, to inspire us to turn to Him and to abide by His laws. God is love, and if we strive to make ourselves more lovable (God-like) we will be making the first step toward changing the world. Someone has said, "Dear God, change the world, and start with me."

Placing God in our hearts is the number one duty of mankind. He made us for the purpose of bettering ourselves and the world. To allow any thing to get between us and Him stunts our spiritual growth. In the words of John Ruskin, "Anything that makes religion a second object makes it no object—he who offers God a second place offers Him no place."

In changing ourselves through religion, we mustn't strive to be more holy than others. Our concentration should be to change ourselves in order to be an inspiration to others, to bring them along, so to speak, by example. After all, "The call to religion is not a call to be better than your fellows, but to be better than yourself" (Rev. Henry Ward Beecher).

The Sacrifice of Christ

According to the Bible, Jesus died on the cross for our sins. I believe he made that supreme sacrifice for another reason as well. He died to further his cause, just as a seed dies to become a tree. In this case it was the tree of Christianity that grew and brought forth goodly fruits. If you plant a seed in the ground a tree will become manifest from it. The seed sacrifices itself to the tree that grows out of it. The seed is outwardly lost, destroyed, but because of its sacrifice, it will be absorbed and embodied in the tree, its blossoms, fruit, and branches. If the identity of that seed had not been sacrificed, no blossoms, fruit, or branches would have been forthcoming.

When Christ, like the seed, sacrificed himself, his personal identity became hidden from the eyes even as the identity of the seed became hidden, but the bounties, divine qualities, and perfections of Christ (the spiritual blossoms, fruits, and branches) became manifest in the Christian community that he founded. Jesus also sacrificed himself as an example for us to sacrifice our earthly desires for heavenly attributes. We must be born again by ridding ourselves of worldly imperfections, becoming purified from selfishness and human desires, and by attaining heavenly graces.

Some folks believe that by accepting Jesus as their Messiah, they are saved for life, being guaranteed a place in heaven. I can't accept that belief. The purpose of being born again is to spiritualize all phases of our lives, and to resist temptations. This is a lifetime job, for although we can work toward perfection, we won't reach it, at least not in this world. What God may accept from us today, He may not accept tomorrow. Thus, each day we must strive to better ourselves. We must be born again day after day.

Faith vs. Belief

I have often wondered why many persons who profess a belief in God are unhappy and distressed. According to the scriptures, true belief in God brings joy and happiness. In Psalm 33:20-21, it is recorded: "Our soul waiteth for the Lord: he is our help and our shield. For our heart shall rejoice in him, because we have trusted in his holy name." In John 15:11 Christ, speaking to his disciples of commandments, told them: "These things have I spoken unto you, that my joy might remain in you, and that your joy might be full." In another place he said: "The thief cometh not, but for to steal, and to kill, and to destroy: I am come that they might have life, and that they might have it more abundantly" (John 10:10).

Some believers do not have the faith to enable them to attain spiritual joy when beset by material troubles. I found a clue to this mystery in the concordance of my Bible, where it describes the difference between "belief" and "faith." It reads: "Belief generally connotes only intellectual assent, while faith implies an accompanying confidence or trust." This statement opened my eyes to the meaning of the story of the two blind men who approached Jesus (Matthew 9:27-29). He asked them, "Believe ye that I am able to do this?" When they answered, "Yea, Lord," he touched their eyes, saying, "According to your faith be it unto you."

An interesting anecdote revealing the difference between belief and faith concerns a tightrope walker who was giving a lecture. He asked his audience, "How many of you believe that I can walk a tightrope across Niagara Falls?" All raised their hands. Then he asked "How many would be willing to sit on my shoulders while I am doing it?" Only one hand went up. This illustrates the difference between belief and faith, and makes clearer the scripture, "For many be called, but few chosen" (Matthew 20:16).

The Necessity of Trials & Afflictions

The mere act of existing brings to awareness the fact that life is a series of tests, trials, and afflictions which occur throughout life. Sometimes when these events occur we may ask, "Why me, God?" Some of these difficulties and troubles are from God, others from man's evil deeds. Ordeals seem to be of two kinds: those which test the soul and those which are punishments for actions. The first is educational and developmental and the second is retribution. I will not dwell on the latter here.

It has been said that God does not lead us into deep water to drown us, but to cleanse us. He wants us to subjugate our material leanings to our inherent (yet often latent) spiritual instincts. To be "born again" we must go through spiritual growing pains. One suffers when one gives up one's self to God. This comes only by sacrifice of the desires of the flesh. The flesh is weak and difficult to overcome, but "he that overcometh shall inherit all things" (Revelation 21:7). Suffering helps to perfect man. When a man is happy he is likely to forget his God, but when grief comes, he either turns to Him or "disowns" Him. (Remember the "God is dead" syndrome?)

Man is like a dull knife that needs to be sharpened to become a suitable instrument to do God's work on earth. If he is flexible, he will become a sharp instrument when placed on the grindstone of life through tests and afflictions. If he is brittle, he will break under the pressures of life's vicissitudes. The grindstone of life is portrayed in Job 5:7, where it is recorded: "Man is born unto trouble, as the sparks fly upward."

Emerson said: "He has seen but half the universe who has never been shown the house of pain." And Shakespeare wrote: "Sweet are the uses of adversity." Although Phil Ossofer is completely out of his class in the above company, he, too, comments on this subject, saying, "When I get in a jam, God jars me, but only to preserve me." Tests, trials, and afflictions can be the best things that happen to us if we understand their true purpose—the development of the soul.

Adversities Help Us Grow

Life is full of adversities, which, in reality, are not meant to be stumbling blocks, but stepping stones. I came to that conclusion when I became aware of God. In fact, it was through adversities that I discovered that awareness. In my younger days, when adversities hit me, I was crushed, moaning, "Why did it happen to me?"

Now I know why "it" happened to me, and I am thankful for these adversities. It was in order to make me come face to face with my shortcomings so that I would struggle with them and overcome them. "Him that overcometh will I make a pillar in the temple of my God" (Revelation 3:12). This is God's way of aiding us to develop the potentialities with which He has endowed us. How can we overcome our weaknesses if God does not make us aware of them? We wouldn't do it on our own.

Adversities no longer threaten me. I accept them as challenges. I used to think of life as being full of ups and downs, but now I see them as downs and ups. That's because I have to undergo before I can overcome.

Just as we develop our physical senses while in the womb so that we can be active in this world, I believe that here on earth we must develop our spiritual senses so that we can be active in the world beyond. My idea of hell would be entering into that world without the necessary senses—the spiritual senses—that would enable me to function there. This is important because that world is eternal, and that's a long time to spend oblivious of that world.

Our shortcomings are more imperfections than sins. The sins come in failing or refusing to try to develop spiritually. Man's most important task on earth is to prepare himself through spiritual development for that world beyond. It is a sin to pass up such a wonderful opportunity.

War With Oneself

God tests all of His children, especially when they make vows to live according to His teachings. In discussing this belief with a friend, I mentioned that since I made peace with God, I have been at war with myself. He considered this a negative attitude for one who believed in God, so I had to explain what I meant by my statement.

I told him that my feeling of being "at war" with myself didn't make me an unhappy, long-suffering person, because a belief in God also entails volition, that is, the will to become a better human being. Such a will, when put into action, causes one to battle consciously one's anti-social habits and prejudices in order to replace them with God-like attributes such as love, cooperation, and service to mankind. This transformation is what we call being born again.

Replacing anti-social habits with good habits is not easy, and when one begins at age forty-three, as I did, one's experiences at times are almost traumatic, because old habits are so deeply ingrained in one's mind, they become natural reflexes. The struggle between what I claimed to believe and my old self brought on a real war in my heart. Slowly, habits are changing, but not without a constant battle. That is why I say that I am at war with myself.

Despite this war, I have found real peace in turning to God, for I know He is a patient, loving Father to all of His children. His compassion surrounds us all. If this were not so, the world would be devoid of human life. Adversities are not sent down upon us to punish us, but to cleanse us. The dual condition of the struggle for self-improvement and the joy in finding God are the agony and the ecstasy of life. Despite the struggle and the suffering for spiritual advancement, the rewards are glorious, for "he that overcometh shall inherit all things; and I will be his God, and he shall be my son" (Revelation 21:7).

Humility

As I read the newspapers and watch the TV news, I become more aware of the growing decadence of our times. I believe this condition is caused by the lack of certain qualities that are necessary for justice and order in the world. Among them are honesty, trustworthiness, and humility, the latter being, in my estimation, the most important of all.

I have often written that our problems stem from men's turning away from God. When this turning away occurs, men become vain and haughty, and in effect, sometimes play God themselves. That is how dictators are made. Humility is an awareness of how little we know plus an acknowledgement of the vastness of the universe and the power of the Creator. It calls for an ever-expanding knowledge of what the Creator has made, giving us the realization of our own powerlessness. For instance, in the time it has taken me to write the above, there have been nearly one billion new red corpuscles created within each of us. Believe me, absorption of such knowledge makes me feel very small!

Without an awareness of a Creator: a super Intelligence, we may become obsessed with a belief that we are very important in the universe.

I believe that humility before God is the key to the door of salvation. Confucius said, "Humility is the foundation of all virtues." There is no way to develop the virtues of honesty and trustworthiness without that foundation. The Bible portrays the high spiritual station of humility. In Proverb 22:4, it is written: "By humility and the fear of the Lord are riches, and honor, and life." And in I Peter 5:5, we read: "And be clothed with humility: for God resisteth the proud, and giveth grace to the humble." The finest examples of humility have been the prophets of God. Although it is impossible for ordinary human beings to attain their holy station, shouldn't we try to emulate them?

Patience

Patience is a much-needed virtue that, for most of us, must be acquired through discipline. Life being what it is, with its trials and afflictions, we may find it difficult to be patient at times. Yet, the very purpose of trials and afflictions is to teach us patience.

The prophets of God are examples of suffering and patience (James 5:10). We would do well to emulate them. The tests suffered with an unshakable faith in God strengthen us in patience. "Knowing this, that the trying of your faith worketh patience" (James 1:3).

We are continually experiencing tests in our daily lives, but it is here that we can best learn patience. In the words of the noted minister of the last century, Henry Ward Beecher, "No man can learn patience except by going out into the hurly-burly world;

and taking life just as it blows. Patience is but lying to and riding out the gale."

We can begin to learn patience by starting with little things. "Learn to bear the everyday trials and annoyances of life quietly and calmly, and then when unforseen trouble or calamity comes, your strength will not forsake you" (Anonymous). Sir Walter Scott wrote: "The sincere and earnest approach of the Christian to the throne of the Almighty teaches the best lesson of patience under affliction, since wherefore should we mark the Deity with supplications, when we insult Him by murmuring under His decrees?" So "Let us run with patience the race that is set before us" (Hebrews 12:1).

Be Guarded In Speech

A little child once asked his mother, "Where do our words go after we say them?" I don't know the mother's answer to this thought provoking question, but I have sought an answer myself.

Some time ago *Readers Digest Magazine* carried an item about an English town in which the local television receivers picked up the image from a Texas station. When some of the viewers wrote to the station it was discovered that it had ceased broadcasting four years before the picture was received on their TV screens!

Where was this picture all that time? I believe this was an as yet unexplainable incident; a physical manifestation of a spiritual law, proving that our words, like our souls, continue to exist beyond this world. Perhaps when we reach the next sphere of existence, our words will be played back to us, an unpleasant thought, considering many of the words I have spoken in anger during my lifetime!

Thus, we must be guarded in our speech, avoiding backbiting, malicious gossip, and unclean subjects. A playback on a spiritual tape recorder in the next world could be one form of hell for us. We would not be able to return to earth to rectify or unsay the unkind and harmful words we may have spoken. We would be in the unhappy condition of the rich man in hell who begged Abraham to send Lazarus to warn his brothers of the same fate

(Luke 16:19-31). Unlike that rich man we are still on earth and still have our free will to do and say what we please. Now is the time to change our speech to words of love and kindness. Such action would be proof of our repentance and may, through the grace of God, save us from having to hear our sinful words again.

So, let us be guarded in our speech, for the hereafter may also be the hear-after.

Cleanliness of Mind

Judging from the ads on television, there is no end of products that help keep one's person and one's home clean. Judging by the increasing sales of such products, people in general must be determined to keep both body and home as clean and as attractive as possible. Strangely enough, however, products offered for people's minds, such as x-rated movies, "adult" books, and some of the fare seen on television, tend to fill one's mind with mental dirt. People are getting cleaner on the outside and dirtier on the inside. It's a sad commentary on today's world.

The importance of how a person thinks is seen in the fact that the mind accepts anything it is offered unless one disciplines oneself to keep degrading thoughts from entering. One must be like a security guard at a nuclear plant, preventing the entrance of anyone who, if allowed in, could destroy the plant. Our "plant," the God-given consciousness, is to last us through eternity, and the state in which we spend that time could well be determined by how we police our minds in this world.

It is a psychological fact that what goes into one's mind eventually comes out in the same form, or remains to attract more of the same, because like attracts like. It is far easier to develop good habits in the first place than to struggle to eliminate bad habits that have taken over because we have allowed bad thoughts to enter the mind for years. If we don't form good habits, our habits will deform us.

Previous to the time I became aware of God and His laws, I

had many thoughts that I wish I had "policed" out of my mind. It hasn't been easy to eliminate those thoughts. Now I can understand to some extent the problems of a drug addict who is on withdrawal. Knowing that many addicts do overcome their difficulties, I was assured that I, too, could completely "withdraw." I am now alerted to that garbage called pornography and how it can contaminate the mind. I liken the mind to the living room of the body. Who would want to keep garbage in their living room?

The Fear of God

There are many things in this country (and in the world at large) that need correcting. If anyone were to ask me to describe a single cure for all of our problems, I would give them the answer in four words: "The fear of God." If mankind as a whole was aware that God rules the world (and the "heavens" too) and that He will judge all in time, men would be honest, non-violent, and loving toward one another. This goal can be reached only through the fear of God.

The Bible is full of reasons why men should fear God. For instance: "The fear of the Lord tendeth to life: and he that hath it shall abide satisfied; he shall not be visited with evil" (Proverb 19:23). Of course, one must first believe in God to benefit from His blessings. "The fool hath said in his heart, There is no God" (Psalm 53:1). If there really were no God there would be no world. There can be no effect without a cause. Every created thing needs a creator, and that creator is greater, more intelligent than that which He creates.

Many men are so deeply engrossed in accumulating material treasures that they have no time to think of God. They go to such great extent with their obsessions that they will do anything, by hook or crook, to attain their goals. Someday, perhaps when it is too late, they will discover that "better is little with the fear of the Lord than great treasures and trouble therewith" (Proverb 15:16).

The Bible reveals the rules for right living. By ignoring God's laws men miss the whole purpose of their God-given lives. Unless they learn what that purpose is, they are in danger of suffering eternal regret. It is only through the fear of God that man can begin to know the destiny for which he was created. "The fear of the Lord is the beginning of wisdom" (Psalm 111:10).

One's fear of God must be like the fear of one's father, who loves his children, and who lovingly but firmly instructs them well. The Bible sums it up: "Let us hear the conclusion of the whole matter: Fear God, and keep his commandments: for this is the whole duty of man" (Ecclesiastes 12:13).

Sacrifice

Self-sacrifice, compassion, and philanthropic deeds, among others, are the heavenly rewards of life. The perfect example was Jesus, who gave his life that humanity might have life more abundantly. Many of his followers suffered martyrdom in his name. In this day, however, it isn't necessary to die for one's beliefs. A martyr today is one who is "dying" to live his beliefs. This is accomplished by sacrificing material things for spiritual things, placing honesty, integrity, justice, and similar virtues first. We needn't give up material things, but we shouldn't let them come between us and God.

If everybody gave up their prejudices and hatreds, the spiritual consequences of their deeds would bring the kingdom of heaven to earth. Although this seems impossible, Jesus said it would happen.

The subject of sacrifice is dealt with in the Bible in reference to money. In Mark 12:42-44, Jesus praises the action of a widow who gave her last two coins ("mites") to the treasury. He said that her contribution was of more value than all the gold given by the rich. I'm sure the consequences of her action were great in heaven. I was so impressed with this parable that I wrote this rhyme:

The widow gave her mite,
Despite her financial plight;
She made a big hit
With her "widow" bit.
It was spiritual dyna-mite!

What Is A "Square"?

What is a "square"? Today it refers to a person who performs his duties to the best of his ability, who gives his best in his work, is more interested in a "work break" than a "coffee break," and who doesn't watch the clock. By modern standards such a person is held in ridicule. "Square" is no longer a compliment.

In days gone by the word "square" had dignity. If one was honest he would give you a square deal. He would stand four-square for right and pay his bills on time, thereby being square with the world. And he would look you square in the eye.

Now, I don't advocate going back to "the good old days," but as I see it, moral laws never change, and they are far more needed today than ever before. If we are to continue living on earth we are going to have to square ourselves with God. We mustn't fall victim to the desires of those whose disdain for square-dealing causes them to cut corners, to look for angles, and to toss us squares some curves. They believe that honesty and God are dead, having lost the true values of life.

Strangely enough, it was "squares" like Nathan Hale ("I regret that I have but one life to give for my country") and Patrick Henry ("Give me liberty or give me death") who helped build this country on four-square principles. But for "squares" such as these, modern rebels might not be here to condemn and ridicule honor and honesty. In other words, if it weren't for such squares as Nathan Hale and Patrick Henry, they wouldn't be a-round!

Material and Spiritual Progress Must Go Together

In this age of great material progress, I see, with dismay, brother turned against brother in hate. It seems strange that although we are becoming material giants, we remain spiritual pigmies.

Christ came that humanity (and I'm sure he meant all humanity) might have life more abundantly (John 10:10). It is impossible for this to be unless the "haves" show compassion for the "have-nots." We seem unaware that God created us all as one family. In reality the family of man is like the human body. We know that if one part of the body is ill or infected, the healthy parts will eventually become affected unless that part is treated and cured. One cannot function normally if the head aches, if an arm is broken, or if the stomach is upset.

Humanity is gravely ill because part of the body of mankind festers with various illnesses, the greatest of which, I believe, is racial prejudice. This is a sickness which should not exist. God's Physician, the Christ, continually proclaimed the remedy: love for all mankind. We avow our love for God, but often belittle our brothers of different colors or beliefs. How can we say we love God, who we have never seen, when we do not love our brother, who we have seen?

Material progress can never last unless spiritual progress goes right along with it. Great civilizations of the past fell because the Great Physician's prescription for living went unheeded. This needn't happen in this age. If we heed God's commandments, treating all with love, and sacrificing self-interest for the well-being of the entire body of mankind, we will not only continue to grow in stature materially, but will become spiritual giants as well.

Possessing Material Things

Living in an age of tremendous material progress, we seek to partake of the endless variety of labor-saving, pleasure bringing devices made available to us. If we lack cash, we buy on credit, just so we may possess these wonderful objects. The question is, do we possess these objects or do they possess us? If we utilize them to ease our labors we possess them. If we use them to indulge ourselves they possess us.

If we drive carelessly, the car possesses us. By being wreckless (not reckless) drivers, we are aware that true possession of the car means using it in the manner for which it was made. If we purchase things merely to indulge ourselves, we will become bogged down in debt. Sir William Temple wrote: "No possessions are good, but by the good use we make of them; without which wealth, power, friends, and servants do but help to make our lives more unhappy."

Guidance in the handling of possessions is emphasized in the Bible: "But seek ye first the kingdom of God, and his righteousness; and all these things shall be added unto you" (Matthew 6:33). By putting first things first (and God should always be first), we will appreciate our possessions and use them properly. Nothing should possess us except God. When we are possessed by Him, we will possess whatever material things we need, becoming their master and not their slave.

This radiant century has brought us more creature comforts than all the previous centuries in known history. Scientists tell us that many more conveniences are in the making, and yet we are just about as uncomfortable as we can be. What's the problem?

I believe it is because we, the possessors of the wonderful "servants" science has provided, have allowed them to possess us. We base our lives on getting more and more, even though we may not be able to afford them, and in doing so, have enslaved ourselves through debt and desire, until we have forgotten the true purpose of life.

God condones the use of creature comforts, but not to the extent that they come between Him and ourselves. This is what is happening today. In our minds we have fashioned of these comforts a modern golden calf to worship, turning from Him who has provided all things for us. On top of this, we have fashioned the idols of racism, nationalism, and religious prejudices, the worship of which debases others of a different nation, race, or creed than ourselves. We have forgotten the first Commandment: "Thou shalt have none other gods before Me."

In the midst of material wealth we suffer because we worship idols. Although not made of stone or gold, they are creations of our idle fancies, which become fancy idols.

How long will this suffering continue? Until we repent and turn away from idol worship (Ezekiel 14:6). If we fail to do this, we will suffer the devastation foretold in Ezekiel chapter 6, so that only a remnant will escape. This is reiterated in the 24th chapter of Matthew, where the calamities we see all about us are described. When we relinquish our worship of materialism, racism, nationalism, and religious prejudice, and turn once again to God, we will be released from the unrest that threatens our world, and will find true liberty, for "Where the Spirit of the Lord is, there is liberty" (II Corinthians 3:17).

Tools to Build the Kingdom

We are living in an intensely crucial age, one such as has never been seen in history. It is crucial because the tools given us by modern science, tools that can be used either for construction or for destruction, are being used more for destructive purposes. This is because man has not yet matured to the point where he will only use the tools of science to build a better world.

Although man has tamed nature, he has not tamed himself. Within man are two natures: a worldly or material nature, and a spiritual nature. Through his free will he chooses either to dominate him. From present world conditions it is evident that too many men, especially those in power, have allowed their worldly nature to dominate them. Man's worldly nature encourages greed, hate, and uncontrolled violence to occur. His spiritual nature teaches him to live in peace and harmony with all mankind, dealing with everyone with justice and compassion.

It is my contention that people in general do not realize what the purpose of life is. With so many material things available, it is very easy to live completely material lives. Many become "couch potatoes." Others grasp selfishly for more and more without concern for the wretchedness under which many of their fellowmen exist. We have been given life to help make this world a better place to live in, so that when we leave it, we will have justified our existence here. The Bible is full of warnings about our material nature. Material things are booby traps that can hinder our spiritual progress. We must not allow them to come between ourselves and God.

The Bible says that man will eventually progress spiritually until he will make this world the kingdom of God "as it is in heaven" (Matthew 6:10). This places a great responsibility on our shoulders, and it is a great challenge to participate in this task.

Who is Rich and Who is Poor?

Who is rich and who is poor? In truth, the answer to this question cannot be discerned on the surface, and is known only to those whose spiritual eyes are open. It is not the lack of worldly goods which makes us poor. It is the lack of spiritual attributes which impoverishes us.

Behold the condition of the beloved Jesus. His food was the grass of the field. His bed the dust, his lamp was the light of the moon, and his steed his feet, yet, who was richer than he? We all thirst for his riches, consciously or unconsciously, for his way is truth.

Jesus said it would be easier for a camel to go through the eye of a needle than for a rich man to get into heaven. Who, then, is poor? Surely not one who lacks worldly treasures, but one in whose heart Christ does not abide.

An appropriate story of riches and poverty is told in Muslim traditions. One of the followers of Sádiq, the sixth Imám of Shí'ah Islam, complained that he was poor. Sádiq said, "Verily, thou art rich, and hast drunk the draught of wealth." His follower, perplexed, asked, "Where are my riches, I who stand in need of a single coin?" Sádiq asked, "Dost thou not possess our love?" He replied, "Yes, I possess it, O thou scion of the Prophet of God!" Sadiq then asked him, "Exchangest thou this love for one thousand dinars?" He answered, "Nay, never will I exchange it, though the world and all that is therein be given me!" Sadiq then remarked, "How can he who possesses such a treasure be called poor?"

The true treasures in this world are the spiritual ones, bestowed upon us when we accept Christ and the other messengers of God in our hearts through our faith and deeds.

Spiritual Bookkeeping

Let's do some spiritual bookkeeping. We'll analyze the books to find out why the world is in its present shape— spiritually flat—and why our moral checks are being returned marked NSF—No Spiritual Funds.

We'll start out with our balance sheet, showing our assets and liabilities. On the asset side are those spiritual qualities latent within us. As our greatest potential, these qualities are deteriorating from lack of use, throwing us off balance toward gross materialism.

On the liability side is the injustice with which we degrade our fellowmen because of the color of their skin or the difference of their belief. When we cancel this debt through equality, we will be out of the red and in the black, financially and spiritually. This debt is the "mortgage" that America has inherited from previous generations, and now it must be paid off.

Now for our biggest job: preparing our prophet and loss statement. We are at a loss because we do not heed our prophets' excellent advice to balance our books with love and unity. In business we listen to our accountants, who direct us toward greater material profits. It is the reverse in our spiritual enterprises. We ignore our CPAs, those Consecrated Prophetic Advisors sent by God to guide us to eternal, spiritual wealth. "Riches profit not in the day of wrath: but righteousness delivereth from death" (Proverb 11:4).

The Day of the Lord, which is at hand, is the Day in which He balances His books: "And the books were opened: and another book was opened, which is the book of life: and the dead were judged out of those things which were written in the books, according to their works" (Revelation 20:12).

The time is short until we will be called to account for the increase in the talents He has given us. In the little time left, let us hasten to improve our works, that we may show a spiritual profit, transforming our spiritually flat world into a spiritually fat world. The dividend we will receive will be the kingdom of God on earth.

The Danger of Material Greed

In this day, success is having the ability to amass as much money as possible, with no regard as to how this goal is achieved. It runs the gamut from selling cocaine to inside trading on Wall Street. So greedy have some become that they are not satisfied with millions, but want to accumulate billions. Truly, as the Bible tells us, "the whole world lieth in wickedness" (I John 5:19).

According to Paul, "the love of money is the root of all evil" (I Timothy 6:10). Men have forgotten the Source of their existence, ignoring God's admonitions that, when obeyed, bring life more abundant on earth and the promise of eternal life. The Bible says that one cannot crave material things and also worship God: "No servant can serve two masters ... ye cannot serve God and mammon." According to the dictionary, "mammon" means "worldliness," "inordinate desire for wealth," "avarice," and "greed."

Jesus knew how the world would be in this day, with its wars and threats of war (Matthew 24:6), when iniquity would abound (Matthew 24:12), and he told us we should not lay up for ourselves "treasures upon earth ... where thieves break through and steal" (Matthew 6:19-20). He foresaw today's prevalent crime. He desired for us to lay up those spiritual treasures in heaven (Matthew 6:20). We should look into our hearts and choose spiritual things over material things, "for where your treasure is, there will your heart be also" (Matthew 6:21).

If we love the world, in other words, anything that comes in between us and God, we cannot love God. In I John 2:15, this is explained: "Love not the world, neither the things that are in the world. If any man love the world, the love of the Father is not in him." If we seek eternal life (and that is the real reason for being on earth), we must remember that "the world passeth away, and the lust thereof: but he that doeth the will of God abideth for ever" (I John 2:17). As for material things, remember that "we brought nothing into this world, and it is certain we can carry nothing out" (I Timothy 6:7).

The Nature of Man

Spirit and Body

We can understand the power of the spirit within each of us by recognizing the limitations of our physical capacities. For instance, when we look around us, we can see only a short distance. But with our inner sight we can "see" the whole world. Now, if the spirit were the same as the body, the inner eye would be limited just like the physical eye. This proves that the spirit is independent of the body.

The body can be compared to a cage and the spirit to a bird in the cage. If the cage is broken, the bird continues to exist. In fact, its feelings will be more powerful and its perception greater. Thus, when the body is broken (dies), the spirit flies free. The spirit becomes "disconnected" from the body and its power becomes stronger.

Again, the body is an instrument and the spirit is the possessor of that instrument. An author has a pen as his instrument. If the pen is broken, the author, as the possessor of the pen, still exists, and he continues to write with another pen. Likewise, when the body dies, the spirit takes on another form ("instrument") through which it continues to exist. We are not told what that "form" will be in the next world, but the Bible says it will be an incorruptible one, unlike the corruptible one we bear in this world. St. Paul said, "For this corruptible must put on

174 *The Bible Revisited*

incorruption, and this mortal must put on immortality" (I Corinthians 15:53). This occurs when we pass on to the next world.

Another example of the power of the spirit can be seen when the body becomes weak or sick, or even if a part, such as an arm or leg, is amputated. Under such conditions the spirit remains in its original state, being eternal. That is why Jesus said, "Fear not them which kill the body, but are not able to kill the soul" (Matthew 10:28).

Two Natures in Man

As a youngster I read the book *The Strange Case of Dr. Jekyll and Mr. Hyde.* This story of a kindly doctor who changed his character into a beastly fiend was, to me, just fiction, with no moral lesson in it. It was only after I became interested in the spiritual aspects of life that I realized it was more than just fiction. In studying religion I discovered that man has two natures—a spiritual nature and a physical nature. In the book, Dr. Jekyll represents the spiritual nature, and Mr. Hyde the physical nature. Man is potentially one or the other, depending on his free will and volition. He can exalt his soul or debase it.

The media abounds with stories of those who choose their "Mr. Hyde" nature over their "Dr. Jekyll" nature. Crime statistics record the multitude of murders, sexual crimes, and child abuse, to name a few. Add to this the persecution of minorities. Some criminals, of course, are sick, but most of them choose their actions consciously. They have forgotten or ignored their Creator, becoming lower than the animals, which act by instinct and cannot distinguish between good and evil. Man's motives are selfishness and willful wrongdoing.

Not all who choose their physical nature and impulses become like Mr. Hyde; however, if not held in rein, those impulses lead in that direction. Today we read of prominent people who are involved in the drug market and of judges who accept bribes. If Diogenes were seeking a truthful man today, he might have a difficult time finding one.

When a human being is born into this world, he has a Dr. Jekyll and a Mr. Hyde latent within him. Perhaps if his earliest environment is wholesome with love and security, he will develop his spiritual or Dr. Jekyll nature. If not, the possibility is great that he might become a Mr. Hyde type.

How to Develop the Higher Nature

Recently I discussed man's two natures, the choice of which can make man either a Dr. Jekyll or a Mr. Hyde. Today I will discuss why man should, and how he can, accentuate his spiritual nature, thereby emulating Dr. Jekyll.

It is quite evident that if the sun did not shine upon the earth, sending forth its lifegiving rays, our world would wither and die. Likewise, if the Sun of Truth, our Creator, did not send His spiritual "rays" (the Holy Spirit) to shine upon men, they could not continue to exist on earth. The Holy Spirit shines continually, fostering spiritual life on earth, and this Spirit is the cause of all physical life as well. Not all individuals feel the full force of those spiritual "rays." Plants, for example, that grow in the shade grow slower than under direct sunlight. Likewise, men who exist in the shade of materialism stunt their spiritual growth. They are like mirrors covered with dross. In such mirrors the spiritual rays cannot reflect God's Light.

As to how we may develop our higher nature, we must become conscious of our station "a little lower than the angels." Man, above all creatures, has been given a soul, which is the power of rational thought. By "connecting" it with the Holy Spirit, we become "born again." The link between the human spirit and the Holy Spirit is the spirit of faith. Unless the human spirit is assisted by the spirit of faith, man does not become acquainted with the divine secrets and the heavenly realities. It is only when we seek to know our Creator by developing our faith that we come out of the shade of materialism. If and when we do so, we leave the womb of materialism and enter the world of the spirit. Our soul (mirror) becomes free of its material dross and begins to reflect the Holy Spirit in this life.

The bottom line is faith. Jesus explained this when he spoke to the diseased woman who touched his garment: "Thy faith hath made thee whole" (Matthew 9:22).

Sin

In religion sin is given great emphasis. It is ordinarily expressed as avoidable evil activity in which human beings are involved at times. My dictionary describes sin as "transgression against the law of God." To me that means deliberate defiance of God's laws. I don't believe that most of us "sinners" come under that heading. More often than not we fall short because of immaturity—a lack of true understanding of certain of God's laws.

Most of us are not deliberately evil. Mankind has been evolving from infancy (spiritually speaking) to childhood to youth to maturity. We should be in the latter stage today. In I Corinthians 3:1, Paul speaks of men as being "even as . . . babes in Christ." He continues:"I have fed you with milk, and not with meat: for hitherto ye were not able to bear it, neither yet now are ye able." In other words, "You are still immature." Paul further explains in Hebrews 5:13-14: "For everyone that useth milk is unskillful in the word of righteousness: for he is a babe." (That's immaturity.) "But strong meat belongeth to them that are of full age, even those who by reason of use have their senses exercised to discern both good and evil." (That's maturity.)

In his book *The Mature Mind,* H. A. Overstreet rejects the concept that we are born in sin. He believes that all come into the world with physical and psychological traces of our ancestors, but that no man starts life so specifically cursed by a will to evil that he is unable to direct his powers toward decency and wholesomeness. Man has free will to choose to follow his lower or material nature or to develop his higher or spiritual nature. In his material nature he lives for the world alone, but in his spiritual nature he turns toward and approaches God. If he lives for the world alone, deliberately in defiance of God's laws, he is sinful, but if he does so because he is not conscious of God, he is a "partaker of milk," and therefore immature.

Salvation

In discussing religion, I often find that people don't make a distinction between being "born again" and being "saved." Many believe that when they are born again they are saved for eternity. Not so, according to my understanding of the Bible.

Being born again means discovering one's true self—the spiritual, eternal self. I believe that being "saved" is a day by day battle beginning at rebirth when, for the first time in one's life, one becomes conscious of the need to perfect one's soul. Thus, one may be saved one day and lost the next, depending on how the battle goes.

The Bible explains that a person who has been born again may fail to be saved. Jesus said, "Not every one that saith unto me, Lord, Lord, shall enter into the kingdom of heaven; but he that doeth the will of my father which is in heaven" (Matthew 7:21). As I see it, doing the will of my heavenly Father means fighting my own spiritual battles and doing the utmost to live by His teachings. In other words, I must add works to my faith.

Rituals, those outward symbols of the inward truth, profit nothing if not accompanied by good deeds. Yes, I may be saved by grace, but I can retain that grace by bringing forth good fruits. We must become, and remain, new persons, "For in Jesus Christ neither circumcision availeth any thing, nor uncircumcision, but a new creature" (Galatians 6:15). The same holds true for baptism, which is not necessary to enter heaven. To one of the thieves who was crucified with him, he said, "Verily I say unto thee, Today shalt thou be with me in paradise" (Luke 23:43). The thief had not been baptised, but his acceptance of his Lord was his spiritual baptism.

If one's heart is fertile soil in which the seeds of the teachings of Jesus are planted, then one is saved. But if one fails to continue to nurture those seeds day by day until they bear fruit, one may fall by the wayside and end up being unsaved.

People keep asking me if I have been "saved," and I answer that I don't really know. I feel that only God knows my spiritual status. Some days I feel as if I am "saved" and other times I'm not sure. To me, being "saved" is a 24 hour a day, seven day a week,

52 weeks a year, lifetime job, with no vacations, but resulting in glorious "retirement" benefits.

Some folks who think they are "saved" may falter along the line, whereas others who may at present be unconscious of their Lord, may be "saved" before they pass on. The Bible gives us examples of both. Judas, an apostle of Jesus, lost his status of being "saved" by betraying his Lord. On the other hand, Saul of Tarsus, an enemy of Jesus, became an apostle of the highest rank. One must admit that, as Saint Paul, he was "saved."

I cannot accept the concept that by merely believing that Jesus is the Son of God, one is "saved" for eternity. Faith without works is dead. We prove our faith through our works. Emerson put it this way: "Do not say things. What you are stands over you the while and thunders that I cannot hear what you say to the contrary." Life is never stagnant. The heart beats constantly, we never stop breathing until we die, and the brain never sleeps. The sun shines always and the earth revolves on its axis with never a pause. The only thing that is permanent in life is change. With change should come improvement. We must become better day by day if we wish to be continually "saved." What God may accept from me today may not suffice for tomorrow, for we should be continually developing spiritually.

The point about being "saved" is that from the moment this wonderful change comes in our lives, we must become changed in our entire attitude toward life, opening the way for further development in an entirely different direction. As I see it, to be continually "saved" means that we must be born again, and again and again, all through life.

The Eternal Realm

Some people have difficulty in believing in life after death. One person suggested that there isn't enough space "out there" for all those who have passed on. I explained to this person that there is no such thing as "space" in the spiritual world. As an example I mentioned the condition of love. The expression "having love in one's heart" doesn't mean that there is a place in the heart where exists love. The heart mentioned in this saying is not the physical heart. It is a symbol used because the heart is the organ that keeps the physical body alive. The "heart" in which love exists takes up no space. It is a spiritual heart containing spiritual attributes.

When the physical heart ceases to function, the body dies. The spiritual heart never dies, nor do those beautiful attributes— love, truthfulness, purity, faithfulness, and holiness. However, these spiritual attributes must be attained while the body is alive, for entering that spaceless kingdom without them would be like entering this world as babes without the senses of this world. One would be spiritually retarded.

The Bible gives the example of five virgins whose lamps without oil prevents them from entering in with their Lord. In a way it is like having an automobile without gasoline. It could not function. I'm sure that those who do not develop those "spaceless" attributes mentioned above would not refuse to put gasoline in the tanks of their cars. That would be foolish. Yet, when it comes to filling their souls—the eternal motive power of man—with the fuel of heavenly attributes, they refuse. That could be eternal foolishness!

I once read a magazine article wherein some biblical experts rejected the concept of life after death. One theologian said, "There is no doubt that the notion of an eternal soul contradicts the biblical idea that the soul is created finite by God." This is a misunderstanding, for although the soul originated in time, i.e. at conception, once it has come into existence it will last forever. That the soul is immortal does not, of course, give it absolute existence, which is confined strictly to God.

Jesus spoke of the "many mansions" he was going to prepare for us after leaving this world. And said, "If it were not so, I would have told you" (John 14:2). Every divinely revealed religion teaches that there is life after death. There are prayers for the dead. What significance could such prayers have if the deceased no longer existed?

It is impossible for me to believe in God without believing in eternal life. Without it there is no possibility of justice. The rewards of this world seem to go, to a great extent, to those lacking in scruples who take advantage of their fellowmen for profit, while the righteous suffer. Indeed, who has suffered more than the prophets of God?

Man's true self is not his physical body. His reality is his spirit, which, if nurtured and developed, makes him the image of God. If God is a Spirit, then man is also a spirit. If God is eternal, it is possible for man to also have eternal life, without which this temporal life would have no real meaning.

We get an insight into the next world when we sleep. As the body lies inert, "dead to the world," so to speak, we dream. In our dreams we speak to others without uttering a sound, we hear without the aid of our ears, and we travel without the slightest motion of our bodies. We may even converse with loved ones who have passed on. Where is the world of the dream? Is it the inner reality of this world, and this world its effect? I am convinced that that world is the real life, and that life on earth is like a dream. Like dreams, this life must end some day. If this is true, what is the purpose of this worldly life? Thackeray said, "Life is the soul's nursery—its training place for the destinies of eternity." To me, as a Navy man, it is the "boot camp" of eternity, full of obstacles planted to train us to the straight and narrow path. All souls will enter the life beyond regardless of their earthly deeds, but a different station will be granted to each according to his works. In the words of Socrates, "All men's souls are immortal, but the souls of the righteous are both immortal and divine."

In this world those who have accumulated riches live in mansions, while the poor live in slums. In the next world, those who accumulated spiritual riches on earth will inherit those many mansions in our Father's house. Since it is easier for a camel to go through the eye of a needle than for a rich man to enter heaven (Matthew 19:24), those who remain spiritually impoverished while accumulating those worldly goods, may exist in the slums of the next world. The Bible speaks of man's injustice and of God's justice. In this world "justice standeth afar off" (Isaiah 59:14). Justice is received by all in the eternal realm. "Great and marvelous are thy works, Lord God Almighty; just and true are thy ways" (Revelation 15:3).

Understanding Death

I attended a seminar on how to combat stress through humor. It was held at the Miami Children's Hospital, basically for nurses, but as a volunteer there, and having a great interest in humor, I felt that I had to attend. The title of the seminar was "I Could Have Died Laughing," and it covered the subject of death.

Of course, death is no laughing matter, in fact, it is traumatic to most, especially when it comes through accident or a dread disease. The humor involved is in recalling the happy memories of the departed. It relieves stress, and is a part of the grieving process. Without it, we might become permanently depressed, as do some survivors.

If we really understood death as the scriptures teach us, our attitude toward it would be quite different. Every religion teaches the same message—that death of the body is not a finality, but the beginning of a more fruitful life in the world beyond.

Hinduism teaches that "Bodies are said to die, but that which posesses the body is eternal, and cannot be destroyed." Zoroaster said, "At death, the soul of the good and faithful man will return to its heavenly abode."

Muhammad stated, "What is life in this world? It is nothing but play and amusement. Best is the Home in the hereafter for those who are righteous." Also, we should remember these words of Jesus: "Verily, verily, I say unto you, if a man keep my saying, he shall never see death" (John 8:51).

Buddhism says, "Death is only the beginning of a new existence." The Bahá'i Faith, which came into being in the last century, concurs with the others: "Though death destroy his (man's) body, it has no power over his spirit; this is eternal, everlasting, both birthless and deathless."

Death is no respecter of persons. It touches us all, but if we live a good and faithful life, as Zoroaster put it, and are true to the words of Jesus, we should have no fear of death. It was my sense of humor that kept stress from affecting me during my 62-day stay in the hospital after open-heart surgery ten years ago, enabling me to overcome fear of death.

Reincarnation

One interesting, but highly debatable subject, is that of reincarnation—the return of a departed soul in another body. As convincing as some reports appear to be, I believe that the soul is on a one-way path, ever progressing forward through those "many mansions" in the world beyond.

One author offers reincarnation as the only choice between returning to earth and oblivion. At the same time she speaks of connections with the world beyond. She proposes that there is a temporary consciousness during the "waiting period" for rebirth in this world.

One person told me that her son had a dream or vision showing him as a soldier landing in a foreign country where his regiment tore down a building near the shore. When he was actually drafted into the army, and sent to Japan at the end of World War II, his regiment did tear down the building he had seen in his dream or vision. He based his belief in reincarnation on this "double" occurrence. I reject his experience as a sign of reincarnation because if he really had, in a previous life, torn down that building, how could it have been standing when he came back a second time?

I knew a devout Christian (whose church does not accept the idea of reincarnation) who had a dream in which her dead grandmother told her that she had been reincarnated in her grandson. She now believes in reincarnation. Although her story sounds convincing, I found what I consider a flaw in it. If her grandmother were really reincarnated in her grandson, how was she able to speak from the world beyond when her soul was supposed to be on earth in him?

It is a fact that no two grains of sand, no two snowflakes, and no two fingerprints are identical. In other words, everything that comes to earth, comes for the first and only time. Reincarnationists believe that we continually return to earth to perfect ourselves, to be qualified to reach Nirvana, or heaven. It seems to me, as I look around, that people are getting worse instead of better.

Those persons who believe in reincarnation—the return of a departed soul in another physical body—include Bible scripture to prove their case. They cite Matthew 17:12, where Jesus says that John the Baptist was Elias, who was to come before the Lord. They believe that it proves that the soul of Elias was reincarnated in the body of John.

John, on the other hand, denied that he was Elias (John 1:21). Both Jesus and John were telling the truth. Jesus was speaking of the perfections of the spirit that were common to both Elias and John, and John was speaking of his own personality. To explain, I will use a flower to demonstrate—a carnation. If I planted a seed last year, and from that seed a carnation grew, and then this year planted another seed and another carnation grew, you couldn't see any difference between them if you saw them side by side. Both would have the same perfume, color, and form, but physically they would be different flowers. Elias and John the Baptist were the same kind of "flowers" spiritually, having different bodies and souls. John came "in the spirit and power of Elias" (Luke 1:17) but not with the same soul. John is not the reincarnation of Elias, nor is this year's carnation a reincarnation of last year's. (Now you know why I used the carnation as my example!)

Reincarnationists believe that Jesus will not return in the flesh, quoting from the New English Bible that the second coming means only the end of one age and the beginning of a new one. However, in the King James version Christ refers to his return as the coming of the "Son of man" (Matthew 24:27). Speaking of the coming of the "Spirit of Truth," Jesus refers to it as "He" six times. This means to me that the coming of the Christ Spirit as another individual will be in the flesh. According to their theory, reincarnationists cannot say that Jesus will return in the flesh because they consider him the Perfect One, who needs not to return to perfect himself.

Religious & Social Issues

Proselytizing

I love my fellowmen, but sometimes this relationship is strained when someone of a different religious belief tries to force his belief on me. In my opinion, there is only one way to come to a decision on a religious belief, and that is through one's own search for and study of different religions. I arrived at my goal in this manner, and respect the rights of everyone else to do likewise.

The first step in such a search can be made if a person is seeking answers about life. I believe there is a time in everyone's life when he or she wonders why life is the way it is. Such wondering is inherent in us, but many are so engrossed in materialism that they don't stop to think and meditate on the meaning of life. Others, who have a certain belief, become so enthusiastic about their belief that they try to force it on people whose beliefs differ from their own. God is love and He doesn't pressure us to believe in Him. He has given us free will to accept, reject, or ignore Him.

I believe that a survey of the "forcers" would show that only a few, if any, came to their belief through their own study of religion. Some have been brainwashed, others' religions have been handed down, accepted blindly without investigation. The God I worship is not narrow-minded. He loves all. Through the voice of Jesus, He told us to love our enemies and "bless them that curse you, do good to them that hate you, and pray for them which despitefully use you, and persecute you" (Matthew 5:44).

Muhammad revealed in the Qur'án (2:257): "Let there be no compulsion in religion." Millions accept him as a prophet of God, but non-believers are not forced to believe in him. Some of his followers, however, have persecuted those of other religions, in disobedience to Muhammad. This is true of all past religions, for history reveals that more blood has been shed in the name of religion than for any other reason. I would suggest that such as try to force their beliefs on others go back to square one and make their own investigation, studying comparative religion. I'm sure they would get a clearer vision of God's truth, which has been revealed in all the religions, and see the irrelevancy of the different rituals and dogmas they contain.

There has been a lot of publicity about Duffey Strode of Marion, North Carolina, the ten-year old boy who was suspended from school a number of times for preaching out loud on school grounds. I admire the youngster's enthusiasm for his religious belief, but I can't condone his method of preaching it.

God is love, so any effort to force one's beliefs on others is wrong. William Penn wrote, "To be furious in religion is to be irreligiously religious." John Donne, an English poet, expressed his belief in this manner: "Christ beats his drum, but he does not press men: Christ is served with voluntaries."

In 1976, I read of a group of religionists who were going from room to room in Jackson Memorial Hospital, disturbing patients and frightening them with threats of damnation. Taking exception to such treatment, I wrote to the editor of the paper, stating (in part) "The true purpose of religious teaching is to plant heaven into men, not scare hell out of them."

Speaking in Tongues

In my study of the Bible one thing that was confusing to me was the "speaking in tongues." Later, after reading about people who spoke "in tongues," and seeing someone on TV who was supposedly doing just that, I began to wonder. Was I lacking in spirituality that I didn't speak in tongues?

Having previously glossed over I Corinthians, chapter 14, where this subject is mentioned, I decided to go back and see exactly what "speaking in tongues" was all about. I found that such speaking was addressed to God, and not understood by man (14:2). This would explain my lack of spirituality by not speaking in tongues.

Coming upon paragraph six, I began to get another picture. Here Paul pointed out the necessity of having understood what is spoken. He said, "Except ye utter by the tongue words easy to be understood, how shall it be known what is spoken? For ye shall speak into the air" (14:9). He indicated that one speaking in tongues should be able to interpret the words (14:13), and although the spirit is praying, the understanding of such speech is unfruitful (14:14).

Although Paul himself could speak in tongues, he said, "Yet in the church I had rather speak five words with my understanding, that by my voice I might teach others also, than ten thousand words in an unknown tongue" (14:19). He warned that by speaking in tongues, others might think the speaker was mad (14:23).

Paul suggested that speaking in tongues should be done by two or three people at most, letting one interpret (14:27), but if there is no interpreter they should keep silent (14:28). By this I would judge that one speaking in tongues, not knowing what he is saying, is voicing meaningless gibberish.

I have no desire to speak in tongues as I understand the term. My devotions would seem meaningless unless I understood every word I used in giving praise to God. The use of language is for fostering understanding between people, not causing confusion by speaking "an unknown tongue."

Liberalism

There is a certain element in religion that thinks that liberalism is a sin. I cannot understand this. The prophets of God were the greatest liberals who ever lived. Jesus came to all mankind, saying, "A new commandment I give unto you, that ye love one another" (John 13:34). How slow humanity is to put this universal teaching into practice.

I see daily an example of this anti-liberalism in a stenciled sign on the wall of a cemetery near my home. It reads: "End the liberal treason," and is embellished with a cross next to it. This religious element teaches hate instead of love, as was commanded by Jesus. Religious liberalism, on the other hand, brings people together in love. To be liberal is to have respect for others regardless of their color, their nationality, or their religious beliefs.

Is it treason to love all mankind? God is love. "If a man say, I love God, and hateth his brother, he is a liar: for he who loveth not his brother whom he hath seen, how can he love God whom he hath not seen?" (I John 4:20). Today, we are not only our brother's keeper, but also our brother's brother. Jesus prayed for the kingdom of God on earth, and promised us the day of the one fold. I am sure that the time will come when his words will be implemented by more and more people, for we are the instruments for God's work on earth. Religious liberals participate in this endeavor, for they desire to see the unity of all mankind and wish to live in peace.

That element in religion that sees liberalism as treason has blinders on its eyes, limiting its vision. Elbert Hubbard, American author and philosopher, explained this situation as "That particular condition where the patient can neither eliminate an old idea nor absorb a new one."

Faith Needs Works

Checking the encyclopedias and almanacs for statistics, we find there are millions of people who profess one religion or another. It is surprising, therefore, that our world is not a peaceful one. After all, the founders of the various religions taught love and came to unify the world. Where have we gone wrong?

An interesting answer comes from a man who was a prisoner of the Tuparmaros (guerrilla terrorists of Uruguay) for seven months. With the Bible as his only companion, he thoroughly studied that Book all that time, and came up with two conclusions: that simple performance of rituals is not enough, nor does an expressed faith without personal performance suffice.

It is evident that many religionists (if we are to believe the statistics) have overlooked these two points. Religionists are supposed to be activists in living a life of godliness for all mankind. Rituals are only outward symbols of the inward truths. An expressed faith without action is faith without works, which, the Bible says, is dead. After all, the only things we really believe in are the ones we act upon. Man is known by his fruits.

The low spiritual ebb in our world today should awaken us to the need to live the religious life. It is because we don't that Karl Marx referred to religion as the opiate of the people. We can (and must) live the teachings of the prophets of God. Our works must exceed our words and we must become spiritually dedicated. This will take sacrifice.

The financial irregularities of religious organizations, PTL in particular, reveal to me that their leaders are not practicing what they are preaching. I cannot reconcile the standard of living of the Bakkers, who led PTL until their recent "dethronement," with true religious living.

The Bible tells us: "Love not the world, neither the things that are in the world. If any man love the world, the love of the Father is not in him" (I John 2:15). To me nothing indicates the lack of love for the Father more than for a man to ask for money in the name of God and then expend large amounts of it for mansions, expensive jewelry and high priced cars for one's own use. Much of that money was given sacrificially by deprived people.

The Arab-Israeli Conflict

The strife in the Middle East between two Semitic peoples, the Arabs and the Jews, is a physical manifestation of Armageddon—the universal battle between the forces of integration and the forces of separation. There are some Arabs and Jews who seek for unity and reconciliation, while others, from both sides, continue to clamor for separation and violent means to eradicate the other group. The means by which the latter seek to obtain their ends is doomed to failure. History has proven that war and conflict, especially in this modern age, are no longer viable answers for solving the disputes between races and nations.

Those Arabs and Jews who plan to uproot each other would do well to ponder the prophecies in their own scriptures. They would find that they have more in common with each other than different. God promised in the Holy Books a great destiny for both Semitic peoples.

Muhammad asked the Arabs of his time why they had not accepted the truth of Moses and Jesus and all the prophets gone before. They could not follow him without first acknowledging the truth of the former messengers of God. Concerning Moses, he said: "And of old gave we Moses the guidance, and we made the children of Israel the heritors of the Book—a guidance and warning to men endued with understanding" (Súra 40:56). Muslim and Christian Arabs should reflect upon those prophecies in God's Book that promise the return of the Jews to Palestine. For example: "Therefore say, Thus saith the Lord God; I will even gather you from the people, and assemble you out of the countries where ye have been scattered, and I will give you the land of Israel" (Ezekiel 11:17). In Isaiah 11:12, we also read of the future assembling of Israel from the four corners of the earth.

At the same time, the Jews in Israel must acknowledge the right of the Palestinians to live there with equal, rights and respect. They should be even as brothers to each other. In reality, they are long separated brethren. Long ago Abraham was promised by God that his son Ishmael (the Father of the Arabs) would beget a great nation, blessed by God (Genesis 17:20). Moses even foretold the coming of Muhammad to his followers: "The Lord thy God will raise up unto thee a Prophet from the midst of thee, of thy brethren [the Arabs], like unto me; unto him ye shall hearken" (Deuteronomy 18:15). If this prophecy had referred to Christ, the term "seed," rather than "brethren," would have been used.

Science & Religion

The true relationship between science and religion is not as yet fully understood, considering the present use of our most powerful scientific development—nuclear power—for purposes of destruction.

This situation brings to mind the allegory of the car and the steering wheel. The car symbolizes science and the steering wheel symbolizes religion. Science (the car) provides the power and religion (the steering wheel) keeps us on the straight and narrow path. In the words of Martin Luther King Jr. ("Strength to Live" 1963), "Science investigates, religion interprets. Science gives man knowledge which is power; religion gives man wisdom, which is control."

In order to control science, religion must be vital. As we see it today, religion has little if any control over science in the direction it is taking. It needs revitalization. Alfred North Whitehead, noted philosopher, described this condition. He wrote, "Religion will not regain its old power until it can face change in the same spirit as does science. Its principles may be eternal, but the expressions of those principles require continual development."

Only God can bring about the changes needed to give religion its old power. It comes through progressive revelation, the updating of religion from age to age. This is a universal age and it calls for universal religion. God knows what we need before we do, and He always provides it. Man takes much time catching up with God's Revelations. It took three centuries before Christianity was accepted as a true religion in Rome.

The Bible speaks of progressive revelation through God's Covenant with Abraham and his descendents. Abraham was ordained to be the father of many nations (Genesis 17:4). Moses, Jesus, and Muhammad were of his seed, and man was promised the "Spirit of Truth," his seed for this age.

With the rapid strides of science today, it is imperative that religion regain its old power. Since God is in charge, I am sure that the "Spirit of Truth" will soon be recognized by all mankind, and will steer science toward a peaceful world.

Evolution and Creation

I believe that science and religion can agree. Science reveals physical truths about the world we live in and religion reveals spiritual truths. Since God created both physical and spiritual reality, both must be true. It is the interpretations of science and religion that cause conflict between the two.

In regard to evolution, if a person can believe that Eve was created from Adam's rib, why should it be so difficult to believe that man existed at one time in prehistoric eras in the shape of a worm? In the earliest period of gestation in the womb, the embryo resembles a worm. In time it progresses from one form to another until it becomes recognizable in the form of a human being, which emerges at birth. This, too, is evolution.

What we should remember is that the embryo is human in its potentiality and character, not animal. It can become a human being, and nothing else. The human embryo might be likened to an apple seed which, although it resembles other seeds, cannot become anything but an apple tree. Such is its destiny. In the same way, the evolution of man on this planet, from his origin until his present form, has always been that of a single species. Evolution does not mean that man evolved from the ape, as some people believe. If there is a relationship at all, it would be a reversal of that process. Consider how many people today are "going ape" and "making a monkey" out of themselves!

I personally can find no conflict between the Bible story of creation and the theory of evolution. The first reveals, in symbolic language, the power of God to create the universe by His Will, and the second tells in more literal terms the physical details of how life developed.

Spiritual Evolution

Years ago, scientists made efforts to find the missing link between the ape and man. They failed because there is no connection between the two. They are different species.

One sociologist stated that he believed that man was the missing link, saying that man is a transitional creature who has failed to fulfill himself as the image of God. He thought that man would eventually exterminate himself and that God would start over to develop a species that would reflect His image, bringing peace and tranquility instead of violence and pollution.

I dispute this gentleman's belief that God has failed in His creation of man. God doesn't make mistakes. He created man with the *potential* to reflect His image, giving him free will to choose the high road of spirituality or the low road of materialism. If man's development to date is a failure, we would not be able to account for persons such as Christ's disciples (not counting Judas), the saints, the lesser prophets and the holy men and women of the Bible, as well as those pure ones of other times and places. There have been true "images" of God throughout history, because certain individuals have chosen the path of spirituality, which has always been available to man.

It is only when one is "born again" that the possibility of attaining the station of reflecting God's image can be realized. This world is the womb of eternal life. An outstanding example of such rebirth is seen in the conversion of Saul of Tarsus into Saint Paul.

Man has evolved physically and at the present time appears to be at the apex of physical development, but he is only at the beginning of spiritual development. He is a material giant, but a spiritual pigmy, on the threshold of spiritual development. Through God's guidance the spiritual evolution of the human species will continue for ages to come.

"Artificial Intelligence"

In the days of yore men tried to build the Tower of Babel with the intention of reaching heaven, which was believed to be somewhere up in the sky. As we look back, we realize that such action was mere foolishness, even though they had meant well. Today there are some who want to build another "Tower of Babel." This time the "builders" are certain scientists who think they will create "artificial intelligence." In other words, they are of the opinion that in the future, computers will be able to make human-like decisions. One scientist said that human beings are "just machines." I wonder, how can a person who is so smart believe that? One does not need to be a scientist to see the fallacy of such a belief. We know that a computer must be programed by a human being. The computer will never be able to create new programs for itself in the way that our minds are able to deduce and analyze new knowledge.

The human body in itself may be like a machine but the power that animates it is not a part of it. Such power (the soul) is a gift from God, and it continues to exist after the "machine" (the body) dies. Science cannot give the computer a soul. I can't imagine a heaven full of computers! The good Lord gave us the ability to create inanimate objects. If we could create life (God forbid!), it would put us on a level with Him. That's a station no human can ever attain.

There is no doubt that the computers of the future will do wonderful things, but they will never have intelligence or express free will. Free will will always be expressed by God-created, living, breathing, intelligent beings.

Mental Illness

We need only to read the newspapers or watch TV to realize that there are many mentally ill people among us. Some of them are the violent ones: mass killers, spouse and child abusers among others. In a sense most criminals are mentally ill; they are persons without a feeling of reality.

Being out of touch with reality means not knowing the purpose of an object. An example (far out, I admit!) is in the case of a person winning a refrigerator in a contest. Unable to understand the purpose of the refrigerator, he stores his boots in it and puts it on his front porch to display it to his neighbors. Not knowing the purpose of the refrigerator, he does not benefit from its essential power—refrigeration.

If a human being doesn't understand the purpose of his own existence, he is out of touch with the reality of himself. In this condition he becomes self-alienated—a word which has become popular as a description of mental illness. One who is self-alienated does not know who he really is or where he is going. He has lost touch with his reality. In this condition his relationships to other human beings will be disturbed and he will be unable to assume responsiblity for himself or for others.

How does one find the purpose of his existence? The answer, I believe, comes from the scriptures. The books of all religions spell out that purpose. In my own mind I would describe the true purpose of life as being to know God and to love Him. To love Him means to obey His laws, brought to us by His prophets throughout the ages.

Suicide

I was surprised to read that suicide is the tenth leading cause of deaths of all Americans, the third leading cause of death among adolescents, and the second leading cause of death among university students. The "experts" have not as yet figured out why these statistics should exist.

Not being an expert myself, I don't know the reasons either, but I believe I know a deterrent for potential suicides. It is a belief in God and in an afterlife. If one knows there is such a future, he would realize that suicide doesn't release him from his problems on earth.

We speak of God as being just. In this world justice does not always prevail, so it must come elsewhere. We speak of God as being merciful. Pronouncing oblivion on His earthly children, to whom He has given the ability to know Him, certainly does not spell out mercy. Jesus said, "In my Father's house are many mansions. If it were not so, I would have told you" (John 14:2).

What has all this to do with suicide? Well, in the first place, one of the Ten Commandments tells us that we should not kill. I believe this includes the killing of one's self. Second, I believe that suicide affects the progress of the soul in the next world. When we were in the womb we developed the physical senses to enable us to function in this world. Likewise, after entering this world, we are given the opportunity to develop the spiritual senses needed to function properly in the world beyond. When we realize the need for this process, we won't be willing to interrupt it by taking our own lives in an untimely fashion. We might be crippling our immortal "form."

Equality of Men and Women

Male superiority is as old as history. It may seem strange, but it is sanctioned and legitimized in the Bible. Although it was God's law at that time, this does not mean that it was meant to be forever. Some laws revealed in scripture were meant only for a certain age.

Christ was condemned by the Jews because he "broke the law" by healing on the Sabbath. However, he said, "The Sabbath was made for man, and not man for the Sabbath" (Mark 2:27). He changed that law because the commandment given by Moses didn't fit the time of Christ, even as the law "an eye for an eye" was no longer valid. It was now time for man to "turn the other cheek."

Likewise, today those scriptures in which Paul places women in an inferior social station are unsuitable for this mature age. Possibly Jesus had this in mind when he said, "I have many things to say unto you, but ye cannot bear them now" (John 16:12). He knew that in the future the promised "Spirit of Truth" would change certain laws even as he did then.

I believe that Paul's remarks, as recorded in the Bible, have encouraged male chauvinism. Here the problem comes from accepting some parts of the Bible while rejecting others. It is possible to recall vividly Paul's statements lowering the station of women and to overlook (or ignore) his statements showing their spiritual equality.

Let us compare two of his statements: (1) "Let your women keep silence in the churches: for it is not permitted for them to speak; but they are commanded to be under obedience, as also saith the law" (I Corinthians 14:34). (2) "There is neither Jew nor Greek, there is neither bond nor free, there is neither male nor female: for ye are all one in Christ Jesus" (Galatians 3:28).

The latter scripture presages this universal age—the age of the oneness of mankind—when the Christ promised "Spirit of Truth" is to guide us into all truth, including full equality between men and women.

Poverty

You have often heard it said that "The poor will always be with us," usually uttered with the thought in mind that it is useless to try to change the situation. You may have seen those bumper strips that proclaim "I fight poverty . . . I work!" Well, I say, "Bully for you, old boy, I work, too, but for the grace of God, I might have been born in the ghetto, growing up with little possibility of bettering my station in life."

It is evident, according to American history, that economic oppression greeted every minority group that migrated to this land, revealing the fact that ghettoes are used to maintain pools of cheap labor by the powers that be. Ghettoes might be compared to concentration camps. Thus, much of our poverty is manmade, and must be dissolved by man, if not through the heart, then through laws.

I do not deny that the poor will always be with us. Jesus said,

"For ye have the poor always with you" (Matthew 26:11). He didn't mean that we should turn away from them. God made the poor for a reason, as a test for the affluent to prove their love for God.

In the Epistle of James 2:2-5, we are made aware of the station of the poor as a test of faith, for God has chosen to make them rich in faith and heirs to the kingdom. Man, however, usually shows favor to the rich, though they may be poor in faith.

In Deuteronomy 15:7-11, we find that we must succor the poor if we are to prosper. Here it is written, "For the poor shall never cease out of the land.... Therefore I command thee saying, Thou shalt open thy hand wide unto thy brother, to thy poor, and to thy needy, in thy land."

Nuclear War

The world is continually beset with the possibility of a nuclear war. Although the danger is imminent, I believe it will never happen. I came to this conclusion from two points of view: the spiritual and the material. The spiritual point of view comes from my understanding of the Bible. Jesus said that we would become as one fold, that God's will shall be done on earth as it is in heaven, and that his words would not pass away until all will be fulfilled. Therefore, the "end of the world" will not be the destruction of the earth, but instead the beginning of "a new earth," a world of peace and tranquility for all mankind.

From the point of view of materialism, I don't believe that Russia plans to destroy the Western World through nuclear bombs. They expect the West to collapse from within, just as Americans expect the Russian system to collapse from within.

As we look back at previous civilizations, we find that most of them collapsed from within. The Roman Empire, for instance, became decadent through a breakdown of morals, through materialism, and the same forms of ungodliness that we can see in our own country today. Greed, causing extremes of poverty and wealth; dishonesty in much of our leadership; the breakdown of family life, which is the basis of a solid civilization; the turning to drugs by a large segment of our population; and pornography, which is considered legal under the present concept of the First Amendment—all of these are taking our civilization on a downward course.

The arms race between the two major powers (America and Russia) is edging out the social needs of the people, and may eventually bankrupt our nation. The ghosts of civilizations past, which raced like lemmings to the sea of disaster, are haunting our great nation. Unless we change the direction we are taking, our civilization will suffer the same fate. Why should Russia want a nuclear war? After all, it would destroy its country, too.